Professionalisation of School Leadership

This book examines the subject of school leadership as a profession. It tackles questions of what it means to be professional and to work within a profession, and how school leadership fits within these definitions.

The book analyses five areas which, in the sociology of professions, are considered important for an occupation to qualify as a profession: knowledge base, education and training, ethics, working conditions, and formation of a professional identity. Based on these criteria, the book offers a comprehensive analysis into a sociological definition of the professional status of school leadership. The authors argue that school leadership is an emerging profession characterised by development and efforts across different areas.

Contributing to the discussion and theorisation of professionalisation, this book will be valuable reading for scholars, researchers, and students in the field of educational leadership and educational policy.

Jakob Ditlev Bøje is Associate Professor in the Department for the Study of Culture, University of Southern Denmark. He teaches in educational studies, and his research focuses on professions, organisations, and leadership in the Nordic welfare state.

Lars Frode Frederiksen is Associate Professor in the Department for the Study of Culture, University of Southern Denmark. He is Director of studies, and his research focuses on organisations and leadership in relation to upper secondary school.

Bjørn Ribers is Associate Professor in the Department for the Study of Culture, University of Southern Denmark. His research focuses on the education and praxis of the European welfare professions, educational science, and professional ethics.

Finn Wiedemann is Associate Professor in the Department for the Study of Culture, University of Southern Denmark. He is director of educational studies. His research focuses on school leadership and current tendencies in pedagogy and education.

Routledge Research in Educational Leadership series

Books in this series

Exploring the Affective Dimensions of Educational Leadership
Psychoanalytic and Arts-based Methods
Alysha J. Farrell

A Model of Emotional Leadership in Schools
Effective Leadership to Support Teachers' Emotional Wellness
Izhak Berkovich and Ori Eyal

Glocalization and the Development of a Hybrid Leadership Model
A Study of Chinese University Presidency
Qingyan Tian

Exploring the Role of the School Principal in Predominantly White Middle Schools
School Leadership to Promote Multicultural Understanding
Jacquelynne Anne Boivin

School Leadership for Democratic Education in South Africa
Perspectives, Achievements and Future Challenges Post-Apartheid
Edited by Tsediso Michael Makoelle, Thabo Makhalemele and Pierre du Plessis

Professionalisation of School Leadership
Theoretical and Analytical Perspectives
Jakob Ditlev Bøje, Lars Frode Frederiksen, Bjørn Ribers, and Finn Wiedemann

For more information on this series, please visit www.routledge.com/Routledge-Research-in-Educational-Leadership/book-series/EDLEAD

Professionalisation of School Leadership
Theoretical and Analytical Perspectives

Jakob Ditlev Bøje, Lars Frode Frederiksen, Bjørn Ribers, and Finn Wiedemann

LONDON AND NEW YORK

First published 2022
by Routledge
2 Park Square, Milton Park, Abingdon, Oxon OX14 4RN

and by Routledge
605 Third Avenue, New York, NY 10158

Routledge is an imprint of the Taylor & Francis Group, an informa business

© 2022 Jakob Ditlev Bøje, Lars Frode Frederiksen, Bjørn Ribers and Finn Wiedemann

The right of Jakob Ditlev Bøje, Lars Frode Frederiksen, Bjørn Ribers and Finn Wiedemann to be identified as authors of this work has been asserted by them in accordance with sections 77 and 78 of the Copyright, Designs and Patents Act 1988.

All rights reserved. No part of this book may be reprinted or reproduced or utilised in any form or by any electronic, mechanical, or other means, now known or hereafter invented, including photocopying and recording, or in any information storage or retrieval system, without permission in writing from the publishers.

Trademark notice: Product or corporate names may be trademarks or registered trademarks, and are used only for identification and explanation without intent to infringe.

British Library Cataloguing-in-Publication Data
A catalogue record for this book is available from the British Library

Library of Congress Cataloging-in-Publication Data
A catalog record for this book has been requested

ISBN: 978-0-367-47084-5 (hbk)
ISBN: 978-1-032-19706-7 (pbk)
ISBN: 978-1-003-03325-7 (ebk)

DOI: 10.4324/9781003033257

Typeset in Times New Roman
by Apex CoVantage, LLC

Contents

	List of figures	vi
	Preface	vii
1	School leadership as an emerging profession	1
2	Professions and professionalisation – a short review	7
3	The knowledge base of school leadership	21
4	Education and preparation of school leaders	37
5	Ethics in school leadership	53
6	Working conditions and work life	66
7	Formation of a professional identity	79
8	Professionalisation of school leadership?	98
	References	105
	Index	118

Figures

3.1 Regimes of practice under New Labour   25
7.1 The actantial model   86

Preface

This book is the result of a coupling between two fields of research: profession studies and studies on school leadership. The authors represent different paths, interests, and competencies in these fields of research, some more established in profession studies and some more established in studies on school leadership. The opportunity to combine these fields of research came from empirical trends in the practice of school leadership: we noticed a tendency to refer to school leadership as a profession and to school leaders as professional leaders. This stimulated our curiosity. Could this really be so? Was school leadership in fact a profession? Compared with teachers, nurses, and social workers, whom we have previously studied, and who have already attempted a path of professionalisation, school leadership is a later and less established occupational group. Therefore, we were sceptical, slightly provoked, but also intrigued by the sudden and unhesitant claim of a professional status to school leadership.

Several research projects and a long tradition of educating and training school leaders at the University of Southern Denmark form the basis for the book. Speaking to and interacting with these practitioners on a daily basis has given us respect of and interest in the lives, actions, and missions pursued by school leaders – individually and collectively. We have never attempted to take up an all-knowing role vis-à-vis these practitioners that tells them what to do in specific contexts; rather, our role is to question, discuss, educate, and respectfully comment on their dispositions. We hope this attempt to remain on our part of the pitch is reflected in the book.

Over the years, we have also learned from other researchers interested in school leadership and in the broader aims of education. This has been through educational leadership networks in the Nordic Educational Research Association (NERA), the Nordic Association of Profession Studies (NORDPRO), and the European Conference on Educational Research (ECER). We have also gained insight from discussions and seminars at the Danish School of Education, Aarhus University, the University of Agder in

Norway, and Uppsala University in Sweden. First and foremost, our own research group – Pedagogy, Culture, and Leadership (PKL) at the University of Southern Denmark – has provided invaluable support in terms of discussing early drafts, raising critical questions, and financing parts of the project. We wish to express a special thanks to the leader of the group, Dion Rüsselbæk-Hansen, and to the former leader of the group, Katrin Hjort.

Our hope is that the book can qualify, further stimulate, and integrate the attempt to professionalise school leadership, both in ways that respect Nordic, democratic, social, and creative aims of education and in ways that allow the individual school leader to perform discretion and do what is in the best interest of their pupils and teachers.

Jakob Ditlev Bøje, Lars Frode Frederiksen,
Bjørn Ribers, and Finn Wiedemann
Odense, July 2021

1 School leadership as an emerging profession

Is school leadership a profession? If so, in what sense of the term and with which implications? In politics, research, and everyday life, the vocation of school leader is frequently referred to as a profession, distinguished and different from that of teachers. School leaders themselves often seem to believe and express their occupation as a profession. Although still a formal member of the unions for teachers in the Scandinavian countries and to some extent in the UK, school leaders have developed distinct associations, identities, and professionalisation strategies that define, for instance, their jurisdiction, knowledge base, and professional ethics (Association of School and College Leaders, 2018; Lederforeningen, 2008; Utdanningsforbundet, 2017). The Danish association of school leaders, Skolelederforerningen, has argued that they are 'a profession in themselves', and they have employed leaders and consultants to spread the news. But does this make them a profession?

The answer to this question depends on the definition of a profession. Existing research on school leadership has used and explored various definitions, but the discussion has been scattered and has fallen short of conceptual clarity. At least three definitions can be discerned, each of which may be more or less prevalent in particular studies on school leadership. In the following, we will introduce these definitions and give examples of how they have been used.

An everyday, a sociological, and an organisational definition of a profession

According to Hjort (2005), to be part of a profession in an everyday understanding, a person (1) performs a job, (2) is paid for that job, and (3) is relatively good at that job. This applies to the professional football player, for instance, who is distinguished from amateurs who are not paid for their efforts and who do not play football particularly well. It may also apply to school leaders in the sense that some are better, or more effective, at their job than others and hence can be called professional. This rather simple understanding is found especially in studies associating the quality of school leadership (being good at one's job) with effect and effectiveness, as measured by student test scores (e.g. Darling-Hammond & Rothman, 2011; Day & Sammons, 2016; Hall, 2016; Leithwood et al., 2004; Murphy, 2005; Pounder, 2011; Robinson, 2011).

A more elaborate definition is found in the sociology of professions, where a set of traits has been developed over the past hundred years. To qualify as a profession, an occupation must exhibit at least the following traits: (1) a formal knowledge base, (2) a long course of education, (3) a code of ethics, (4) autonomy in work and thus possibilities for discretion, and (5) shared identity and language (Abbott, 1988; Larson, 1977; Millerson, 1964; Parsons, 1968; Weber, 1978). This definition occurs mostly in studies where the notions of profession and professionalism are placed centre stage, and school leadership is compared to and analysed in terms of these (e.g. Cranston, 2013; Keddie, 2017; Ottesen, 2016; Weinreich, 2014).

A third definition is called the organisational definition (Evetts, 2003, 2011; Kipping, 2011; Mik-Meyer, 2018; Waring & Currie, 2009). It revolves around the market and the strategies and standards of the organisations in which most of today's professions work. To be a profession according to this definition means adhering to the business plans and standards of private and/or public enterprises, including the whims of individual leaders. In this understanding, professions are not self-governing bodies responsible only to their own collegiate control and to state regulation. Cranston (2013) has applied this definition vis-à-vis a definition of occupational professionalism, which is the definition given above by the sociology of professions. He argues that school leadership should be responsible to occupational professionalism and not accountable to organisational professionalism. Similarly, other studies point out the relation between accountability and New Public Management, and, in doing so, they articulate organisational professionalism as a political intervention, a kind of New Public Management-professionalism, which, in fact, is de-professionalising according to the sociological definition (Eacott, 2011; English, 2000, 2006; Gunter & Forrester, 2009; Moos, 2013).

In this way, various articulations and discursive remakings have occurred since the development of this sociological definition of professions. This is evident in the everyday language, in politics, in the media, and in research. Depending on the definition chosen, school leadership may or may not be seen as a profession.

Aim of the book

In this book, we will employ the sociological definition and argue that, from this point of departure, school leadership does not (yet) qualify as a profession – at least not as a full-fledged profession similar to the first and classic professions: the priesthood, medicine, law, and engineering. It may possibly qualify as a semi-profession or an emerging profession similar to the later and less established groups, such as teachers, nurses, and social workers. The question then is to what extent and in what ways can school leadership be regarded an emerging profession? Is the occupation more developed in some respects than others – for instance, the knowledge base and education versus ethics and autonomy? What endeavours are needed to develop the profession, and what are the implications of this professionalisation project (Larson, 1977)?

We will attempt to answer these questions in this book. We will do this theoretically, as well as analytically, using empirical material and examples from a series of current or recent research projects (Hansen & Frederiksen, 2017; Hjort et al., 2018; Wiedemann, 2019). We will also base our analysis on existing research.

The special feature of this book is that we will add and combine more than one or two traits in our analysis and discussion of school leadership as a profession. The existing research shows a common tendency to focus on one or perhaps two traits/themes at a time and, from there, develop more general assumptions about school leadership. We will combine two fields of research which are usually distinct, namely (1) profession studies and (2) studies on school leadership. Our references, and the book in general, will reflect this combination.

On the one hand, this combinatory method is the strength and uniqueness of the book. On the other hand, we recognise this method is also a weakness. Covering so much in a short collection is difficult, and the themes and fields of research are usually kept apart for a number of reasons. Nevertheless, we take a bold step forward here. The success of our endeavour must be judged by the reader.

Contents

The book consists of eight chapters which analyse and discuss professionalisation of school leadership within five themes. These themes are derived from the sociological definition of professions – more precisely, from the five traits mentioned above (see also below). We realise society has changed since these traits were developed, and circumstances, such as marketisation and New Public Management, play unprecedented roles in determining how professionalisation projects can be realised in the current context. Nevertheless, we choose to analyse school leadership according to the sociological definition. We do this because we want to compare this occupation and its norms and values to those of other previous occupations that have aspired to achieve professional status – teachers, nurses, social workers, and so on (e.g. Etzioni, 1969). We also choose this definition because it is the one that is best grounded in research and academic discourse. The everyday and organisational definitions are more grounded in common and political discourse, and we do not find this a suitable point of departure for the present analysis. These definitions allow almost any occupation to declare itself a profession, with no further analysis, reflection, or questions required. We believe school leadership deserves to be asked some questions, even if the professional associations have already declared themselves a profession.

The eight chapters in the book are the following:

1 *School leadership as an emerging profession.* Here, we describe the purpose, content, and method of the book.
2 *Professions and professionalisation – a short review.* In this chapter, we review the sociology of professions and the organisational definition in more detail. As such, the chapter lays a foundation for the subsequent and more analytical chapters.
3 *The knowledge base of school leadership.* In this chapter, we analyse the knowledge base of school leadership. This includes considerations of the tacit and abstract knowledge used in the practice of school leadership. Furthermore, we analyse the variations in research on this question. Leadership research – and leadership in general – is characterised by many competing perspectives regarding theoretical foundations and methodological approaches. Therefore, whether something like a knowledge base in fact exists is questionable.
4 *Education and preparation of school leaders.* In this chapter, we analyse the education and training programmes of school leaders in Denmark, as well as in other countries. In analogy to the previous chapters, we ask what knowledge these programmes are based on, who offers and designs these programmes, and what are future school leaders trained for by these programmes.
5 *Ethics in school leadership.* In the case of school leaders, ethics is closely connected to the purpose of the school – which, in Denmark, is democratic formation (Bildung), as well as basic education. Have codes of ethics been developed which reflect these purposes? Are the codes followed, and does that make school leadership an ethical affair? How is ethics balanced next to the demands of accountability and marketisation? This chapter addresses these questions.
6 *Working conditions and work life.* In this chapter, we focus in part on the working conditions of school leaders and in part on the everyday practicing of school leadership. Professional work is characterised by relative autonomy and possibilities for discretion, but do school leaders

have these possibilities? What is left for them to decide if economy, politics, and governance define the room for manoeuvring?

7 *Formation of a professional identity.* In this chapter, we explore the formation of professional identities among school leaders. A common dilemma for school leaders is how to balance their former identity as teachers with their new identities as leaders. The chapter provides examples of how this can be done, and these examples are discussed in relation to the overall question of professionalisation of school leadership.

8 *Professionalisation of school leadership?* Finally, we gather the threads from the previous chapters and attempt to arrive at a conclusion regarding the extent to which school leadership is an emerging profession.

The chapters may be read individually or in a sequence in which the analysis gradually progresses.

A word on sources, terms, and the range of the book

Having described the overall approach of the book and some of its limitations, we feel that a few extra words on the sources and terms used are appropriate. We hope this will also clarify the range of the book.

As mentioned, the book is based on current and recent research projects (published, for example, in Hansen & Frederiksen, 2017; Hjort et al., 2018; Wiedemann, 2019). This means our examples and immediate frame of reference are derived from a Danish context. From here, we have made efforts to include examples and research from other Nordic countries and, ultimately, Anglo-Saxon countries.

Some chapters (5, 6, and 7) are based on Danish examples and Nordic literature to a greater extent than the others. Chapters 2, 3, and 4 are reviews that draw substantially on literature from the UK and USA. This is partly because the field is international. To become a recognised member of this field, even in the Nordic countries, reference to the English literature is key. We have sought to strike a balance when the Nordic context is our point of departure and the Anglo-Saxon countries our extended purview. This plays out in a fashion whereby the first chapters are reviews and 'English', while the later chapters are more empirical, exemplary, and based on the Danish/Nordic literature.

By the term 'review', we do not mean a systematic review based on a short time span and where everything is included. Rather, we mean a narrative review, where the gradual understanding of the theme in question is the guiding principle and determinant of what is included and excluded (Rhoades, 2011). We begin by taking a new look at our own research, and we then conduct searches in well-known databases (e.g. ERIC and Web of Science). In between these efforts, we studied the references of other works. This method, which is a chain search of sorts, allowed us to identify the networks of specific authors. We have looked for the research groups they typically reference, and the ones they do not reference, and we have been surprised to see the apparent separateness of specific networks. This indicates competing positions in particular fields. In Chapters 3 and 4, on the knowledge base and education, respectively, we identify dominant and dominated positions – the so-called orthodoxies and heterodoxies.

Throughout the book, we use the term 'school leadership'. This term is used interchangeably with other terms and notions, such as 'educational leadership', 'headship', 'principalship', and 'administration'. Historical reasons may explain why particular terms are preferred in some contexts (e.g. 'administration' in the USA), but we will not go into that in this book.

We also take a broad view on different levels of the education system in which school leadership is exerted. Most of our examples are derived from the Danish basic school, but the analysis applies to upper secondary school as well. It is more difficult to extend the analysis to the two extremes of the education system – kindergarten and university.

2 Professions and professionalisation – a short review

As mentioned in the introduction, the current discussion and research on school leadership draw on a number of definitions regarding the nature of professions: an everyday definition, a sociological definition, an organisational definition, and perhaps more. This chapter reviews the sociological and organisational definitions. The everyday definition is omitted because we do not find it an appropriate point of departure for our analysis. It draws on conflicting and too politicised discourses. In later chapters, we exemplify how the everyday understanding permeates into some of the research on school leadership, and we will discuss implications of this.

The aim of this chapter is to provide an overview and lay a foundation for the subsequent and more analytical chapters, where specific themes and traits from the sociological definition are studied in detail. The literature and mode of presentation are chosen based on this aim. We have omitted some contributions, especially in the latter part on the organisational definition, in exchange for clarity, structure, and historic perspective.

The sociological definition

The sociological definition typically involves a set of traits that the occupation in question must exhibit in order to be considered a full profession. This so-called 'trait analysis' usually includes the following: extensive education, a formal knowledge base, technical skills, a work ethic dedicated to the public good, a shared identity and language, professional organisation, autonomy in work, collegiate control, certified authorisation, and societal recognition (Durkheim, 1957; Etzioni, 1969; Goode, 1957; Millerson, 1964; Parsons, 1951; Wilensky, 1964).

However, trait analysis is merely one branch of the sociology of professions. It is related to a broader strand of research and scholarly work which will be referred to here as the functional approach. This approach is usually the opposite of a power approach. Next, both approaches will be elaborated upon within the overall frame of the sociological definition.

The functional approach

The functional approach is associated with Talcott Parsons (1951, 1954, 1968), his notion of the social system, and his generally optimistic view of professions. Durkheim (1957, 1984) is another proponent who is often quoted for his essay on *Professional ethics and civil morals* (Durkheim, 1957). Both can be regarded as predecessors to the later trait analysis. To characterise these theories, and thus to recall what may since have been forgotten or neglected in trait analysis, we will enlarge on the most prevalent view – namely, that of Talcott Parsons.

Talcott Parsons

To begin with, the context of Parsons' work is important to consider. In the 1940s and 1950s, Parsons was concerned about 'restoring' American sociology and disentangling the discipline from economics and behaviourism (Camic, 1992). Parsons had trained as an economist, so he departed from the utilitarian dilemma: how can there be order in society if everyone, as the utilitarian doctrine states, is preoccupied with their own self-interest? What prevents chaos from erupting? To pursue this question, Parsons had to break with economics as a discipline resting on utilitarian and rational choice theories. The same applied to behaviourism (e.g. social behaviourism in the shape of the Chicago school), which, according to Parsons, reduced human conduct to questions of behaviour (Hamilton, 1992).

To break with economics and behaviourism, Parsons founded his theoretical framework on voluntarism accompanied by systems theory. On the one hand, humans have a free will and are free to pursue goals other than economic ones. On the other hand, human action is mediated by societal norms and values. Thus, a reciprocal relation exists between individuals and society. This new perspective could explain the utilitarian dilemma: humans are not, first and foremost, self-interested but are instead interested in fulfilling social norms and values internalised via socialisation. Humans are interested in social order, not chaos.

According to Parsons, professions and professionals were particularly important institutions for the maintenance and reproduction of societal norms and values. In this sense, professions and professionals were key parts of society which was viewed as a social system in which every part plays a clearly delineated role. Their professional ethos expressing a client orientation (i.e. an orientation towards service, altruism, or social welfare) reflected and may still reflect this basic orientation to principal values of society. This distinguishes the professional from the businessperson; the professional, as part of a social contract with society, achieves a suitable salary in recognition of their services, whereas the businessperson is paid in cash for their job (Parsons, 1951, p. 435). Whether this is in fact true, or whether other, more complex relations exist between professionals and businessmen, as altruistic and egocentric motifs, remains one of the central discussions in today's research on the professions.

Based on this functional approach, Parsons developed a number of role-specific characteristics to describe the professional.[1] These are:

- High technical competence
- Universalistic
- Functionally specific
- Affectively neutral

(Parsons, 1951, pp. 434–435)

These characteristics would later be developed by trait analysis. In Parsons' interpretation, the characteristics are developed through a demarcation of traditionalistic forms of competence and legitimation. Parsons draws on Weber's distinction among traditionalistic, charismatic, legalistic, and rational forms of legitimacy (Weber, 1978, 2008), as he generally did in his attempt to restore American sociology as a theoretical and not merely an empirical discipline. As opposed to shamans, witch doctors, chiefs, or elders, the professional holds a high technical competence based on abstract knowledge and university training. Furthermore, the professional is universalistic in the sense of not distinguishing among clients based on their wealth, ethnicity, religion, and so on. Functional specificity means that the professional may be consulted in specific matters – as a doctor, lawyer, or engineer, for example – but not in all matters. Affective neutrality further requires an objective stance regarding social and human problems (e.g. sickness, divorce, finances).

This characteristic shows that the professional is clearly associated with norms and values, such as rationalism, equality, and democracy, that are key to modern society. However, the demarcation of traditionalistic forms of competence and legitimacy seems to pull the professional into a more technical direction in which effectiveness becomes a goal in itself. This paradox creates a tension in Parsons' sociology of the professions. In his most famous and encyclopaedic text, Parsons (1968) puts an even stronger focus on abstract knowledge and expert training, as represented by the universities. Thus, the technical pull seems reinforced compared with his earlier works, which had more focus on societal norms and values.

10 *Professions and professionalisation*

Overall, Parsons should be read as a theoretical and macro-oriented interpreter of the professions. Their role in society is what is important, not the traits in themselves. This point seems to be forgotten in the ensuing trait analysis.

Trait analysis

In his essay, *A community within a community: the professions*, Goode (1957) develops eight characteristics of a profession (not a *professional*, as in Parsons' case). The characteristics are:

> (1) Its members are bound by a sense of identity. (2) Once in it, few leave, so that it is a terminal or continuing status, for the most part. (3) Its members share values in common. (4) Its role definitions vis-à-vis both members and non-members are agreed upon and are the same for all members. (5) Within the areas of communal action there is a common language, which is understood only partially by outsiders. (6) The Community has power over its members. (7) Its limits are reasonably clear, though they are not physical and geographical, but social. (8) Though it does not produce the next generation biologically, it does so socially through its control over the selection of professional trainees, and through its training processes it sends these recruits through an adult socialization process
>
> (Goode, 1957, p. 194).

To some extent, these characteristics overlap with Parsons' characteristics – for example, in terms of values shared by all members and in terms of training and competence. However, Goode puts more emphasis on the seclusive nature of a profession, as a community within a community. Becoming this type of community requires a sense of shared identity and language and limits outsiders. Furthermore, training and socialisation add to the sense of community and identity and do not merely equip the professional with technical competence.

In Goode's description, this becoming a profession seems legitimate. It is not interpreted as an instance of power or social closure, as the power approach would explain it. Rather, Goode views the professions as a kind of vanguard of the industrialisation of the USA (Goode, 1957, p. 195).

Millerson (1964) emphasises the following six characteristics of a profession:

1   A profession involves a skill based on theoretical knowledge.
2   The skill requires training and education.

3   The professional must demonstrate competence by passing a test.
4   Integrity is maintained by adherence to a code of conduct.
5   The service is for the public good.
6   The profession is organized.

(Millerson, 1964, p. 4)

Millerson is especially interested in the last characteristic – the organisation of a profession. The title of his book, *The qualifying associations – a study in professionalisation*, indicates his interest in the process, in which approximately ' one hundred and such associations' were involved at that time in the UK, striving for status as full-fledged professions (Millerson, 1964, p. IX). As such, his is more a book on professionalisation than on professions and professionals. According to Millerson, occupations such as teachers, social workers, architects, and bankers could quite likely qualify as a profession one day. Lack of success could mainly be attributed to failing to organise the occupation properly –that is, by not following the distinctive traits of the classical professions (priests, doctors, and solicitors). That this path also involves the struggle over power, the exclusion of some, and the inclusion of others is not discussed in his account.

Etzioni (1969) and Wilensky (1964) take up the same theme and study professionalisation among occupations which do not (yet) qualify as full-fledged professions according to the developed traits. The question is: will these occupations develop into 'real' professions if they follow the path laid out by the classic professions, or is this impossible and futile? Wilensky thought it possible in step with the generally increasing levels of education and expertise among the Western populations. Etzioni and the contributors to his anthology were more sceptical. In the case of teachers, Lortie (1969) discussed, on the one hand, their organisation and high level of autonomy as traits which could speak in favour of teachers one day evolving into a 'real' profession. On the other hand, the 'chronic demand' of teaching and teachers in modern society means that teachers are unlikely to have control over the selection and training of candidates. The state will typically interfere; thus, teachers seem destined to remain a semi-profession according to this criterion.

Although not preoccupied with developing traits of professions and professionals, Millerson, Wilensky, and Etzioni still depart from these traits when assessing other and similar occupations. Thus, they can be viewed as part of the trait analysis and as profession-friendly or profession-affirmative contributors. The extent to which the trait analysis considers and describes professions as part of society, as fulfilling a role in society, can be discussed. Generally, the attempt is poorer than in Parsons' case. This may reflect the incurrence of a normative dimension: the attempt is not simply to describe and analyse, but also to assess if other and more recent occupations could become full professions. However, in both Parsons' analysis and the trait analysis, professions, professionals, and professionalisation tend to be treated as ahistorical phenomena expressing essential traits of society and groups within society. In this respect, the power approach differs.

The power approach

Max Weber

Max Weber is usually perceived as the founding father of the power approach. Like Parsons, Weber did not study professions exclusively but as part of the emergence of modern society from the beginning of the 20th century. This era was marked by an erosion of religion and tradition and, in turn, the adoption of new notions of rationalism, bureaucracy, mass democracy, and state building. In response, professions such as the modern priesthood, the military, and law advanced. Thus, bureaucracy and professions became each other's preconditions, not antithetical, as is often assumed in today's discussion of New Public Management versus the professions (e.g. Ackroyd et al., 2007; Brante et al., 2015; Mik-Meyer, 2018).

To Weber, bureaucracy arose as part of an attempt to control the modern state more effectively. Bureaucracy is often not associated with effectiveness (rather the contrary), but, to Weber, bureaucracy was a highly effective and rational way of organising work. This was viewed against a backdrop of the 'ancient regime', in which nobles took up influential posts as part of an honorary agreement with the king and as a sideline activity. The king provided land and honour, while nobles provided advice, support, and armoury in times of war. In contrast to this agreement, the civil servant in the modern state or the soldier in the modern army is typically an employee with a formal (lifelong) contract, a regular income, a pension, and so on. This makes the system less fragile and more effective, according to Weber. Weber even compared a fully operational bureaucracy to a machine that is characterised by precision, swiftness, unambiguity, documentation, continuity, discretion, uniformity, hierarchy, smoothness, and reduction of personal and professional costs (Weber, 1978, pp. 973–975).

More specifically, bureaucracy is characterised by a series of ideal-typical traits which also mark the civil servant and ultimately the professional. These are:

1 Legitimation via rationality as opposed to legitimation via tradition (personal authority) or charisma (heroism). This implies rules

expressing an order of command and, following this, obedience among subordinates.
2   Hierarchical organisation
3   Clearly demarcated jurisdictions, often referred to as official duties
4   The use of documents to build up cases
5   Professional training
6   Selection of candidates via university diplomas (Weber, 1978, pp. 956–958)

The professional is further elaborated through a series of distinctions between different occupations, first and foremost the priest and the magician. The priest is distinguished by 'his professional equipment of special knowledge, fixed doctrine, and vocational qualifications' (Weber, 1978, p. 425). By contrast, the magician or sorcerer is described as irrational, selected by means of tradition and inheritance and trained in empirical lore and personal awakening. Furthermore, touching on the dimension of power, the priest is legitimised via rationalism and knowledge (doctrine), whereas the magician receives his authority through charisma, revealed in miracle and ritual.

Whereas Parsons, as a translator and transmitter of Weber's work, viewed such traits positively as signs of modernity, rationalism, and progress, Weber was more sceptical – hence, the association with the power approach. On the one hand, bureaucracy and, more generally, modernity were pivotal for breaking with the ancient regime and for democratisation, while, on the other hand, the dawning attempts at democracy were interpreted critically as the rise of mass democracy and politics as a vocation. That is, exclusionary practices were invoked in which membership and success were determined by knowledge and competence, not opinion and representation. Following this, Weber did not simply interpret education, training, exams, and formal knowledge as signs of progress but as means of social closure and monopolisation:

> If we hear from all sides demands for the introduction of regulated curricula culminating in specialised examinations, the reason behind this is, of course, not a suddenly awakened 'thirst for education', but rather the desire to limit the supply of candidates for these positions and to monopolise them for the holders of educational patents.
> (Weber, 1978, p. 1000)

Thus, Weber regarded the modern education system, based on formal exams instead of privileges and hereditary selection, as institutions for the reproduction of the ruling classes. The same applied to the professions. Entrance to both was de facto not democratic but determined by economic and cultural resources. Furthermore, the honorary principles characterising the distribution of power in the ancient regime did not wither away in the transition to modernity; instead, they were transformed, for example, as ethics and ethos in the professions. The cultural values which, according to Parsons, gave legitimacy and privileges to the professions were, to Weber, a substitute for a divine ruler who serves the purpose of dignifying the work of the civil servant.

Neo-Weberians

Weber's view on the professions has been elaborated by the studies of a more recent group often referred to as neo-Weberians. However, Weber is not the sole reference in these critical studies. This thinking is also connected to Marx, feminism, the Chicago school, etc.

Terence Johnson (1972) was among the first to develop Weber's idea of social closure. He did so by reinterpreting the traits developed by Parsons and the trait analysts. These do not describe an inner quality or essence of the professions/professionals but are rather the means necessary for the control of an occupation. Thus, a profession 'becomes redefined as a peculiar type of occupational control rather than an expression of the inherent nature of particular occupations. A profession is not, then, an occupation, but a means of controlling an occupation' (Johnson, 1972, p. 45). In line with this, abstract knowledge is reinterpreted not as a means to improve practice but as a power tool to increase social distance between the practitioner and client:

> The power relationship existing between practitioner and client may be such, then, as to enable the practitioner to increase the social distance and his own autonomy and control over practice by engaging in a process of 'mystification'. Uncertainty is not, therefore, entirely cognitive in origin but may be deliberately increased to serve manipulative or managerial ends.
>
> (Johnson, 1972, p. 43)

Uncertainty in the practitioner–client relationship therefore appears not only due to the fact that the practitioner possesses knowledge the client does not, but also because abstract knowledge is used deliberately in a process of 'mystification'. Through this interpretation, Johnson seems to take a step back compared with Weber and re-associates the professional with the magician. Weber did not make a sharp distinction between the magician and the professional; however, compared to Johnson, his interpretation was more profession-friendly on this point.

Professions and professionalisation 15

Focussing more on the historic process through which the classic professions emerged in the UK and USA in the beginning of the 19th century, Larson (1977) developed a notion of 'professional projects' to establish the tactics, connections, and credentials used by specific groups of the bourgeoisie. Like Weber, she puts emphasis on the role of the modern university, which was invented by the relevant groups and equipped them with the credentials necessary for becoming professionals. In Bourdieu's terms, it was the means of transforming the nobility into a state nobility (Bourdieu, 1996). This social reproduction was only possible in a specific era, however. According to Larson, the liberal phase of capitalism rendered possible a structural model for the creation of the classic professions. Opposed to this is today's version of professionalism and professionalisation among the so-called semi-professions: nurses, teachers, social workers, and perhaps school leaders. According to Larson, no structural model exists for these professional projects to fit into. Instead, they tend to function as myths or ideological forms of control that reproduce the traits and paths of the classic professions without a view to success.

Another group of neo-Weberians (Murphy, 1988; Parkin, 1979; Witz, 1992) developed Weber's concept of social closure by studying not so much education but inter-professional relations, class cleavages, and power tactics in organisations of work – for example, the modern hospital. Following Weber, Parkin describes social closure as:

> the process by which social collectivities seek to maximise rewards by restricting access to resources and opportunities to a limited circle of eligibles. This entails the singling out of certain social or physical attributes as the justificatory basis of exclusion.
> (Parkin, 1979, p. 44)

However, this type of social closure merely describes the dominant and exclusionary closure strategy used by dominant groups vis-à-vis subordinate groups. In addition, Parkin describes two closure strategies 'adopted by the excluded themselves as a direct response to their status as outsiders' (Parkin, 1979, pp. 44–45). These are (1) usurpation and (2) dual closure. In the first case (usurpation), a subordinate group seeks influence and power from a dominant group through an upward, countervailing exercise of power. In the second case (dual closure), the strategy aims at both usurpation (upwards) and exclusion (downwards).

Witz (1992) has applied these concepts to the study of inter-professional relations in the medical field and is one of the few to focus on the sociology of professions and gendered divisions of labour. She describes how closure strategies are in fact gendered strategies, in the sense that exclusionary tactics are primarily used by men, while usurpation and dual closure strategies pertain to women. As examples, Witz describes strategies used by male doctors and female nurses. In the first case, male doctors have, for example, played a role in barring women from universities until the middle of the 19th century, thereby preventing them from entering the medical profession. In the latter case, nurses have, as Florence Nightingale-figures, taken over some of the functions rendered superfluous among male doctors (usurpation) and, more confrontationally, have used legalistic and credential tactics aimed at both doctors and auxiliary personnel (dual closure). Furthermore, with inspiration from Larson (1977), Witz argues that female professional projects must mobilise 'proxy male power' in order to become successful (Witz, 1992, p. 201). This is typically achieved by employing men as leaders of the professional associations or by adopting science and 'hard knowledge' to dissociate women from images of care and other 'soft' competencies. In this way, female professional projects tend to be paradoxical.

Lastly, Freidson (2001) and Abbott (1988, 2005) can be regarded as a branch of neo neo-Weberians who focus more closely on boundaries and divisions of labour in a system of professions – in Freidson's case, the medical field, and in Abbott's case, among 'linked ecologies', such as psychiatry and psychology. They moderate some of the critique and power perspectives characteristic of the neo-Weberians and take over some of the self-perceptions and models of contemporary professions. Abbott, for example, stresses what, in his view, seems to be a legitimate mode of becoming a profession, namely via jurisdictional claim. Jurisdictions are similar to monopolies but are interpreted less critically as relations between a field of work and an occupation claiming to perform this work better than other occupations. Legitimacy is attained by social, cognitive, and cultural dimensions of the jurisdictional claim (e.g. the knowledge and competencies distinguishing professionals from laymen). Still, Freidson and Abbott are mentioned within this critical branch of the sociology of professions since they also emphasise the boundary work and power tactics employed by groups of professions within systems of professions.

Whether any 'real' profession or professional is *either* a functional and good project/person *or* a power-seeking and bad project/person remains in question. A more likely scenario is that professions and practitioners mix these qualities and attain a position along a continuum of altruism and power. Some may be more altruistic than others, however.

The organisational definition

The organisational definition revolves around the fact that professionals increasingly work in large organisations operating in global markets and

Professions and professionalisation 17

setting the agenda for the performance of work. Furthermore, the organisational definition exploits and contributes to the dissolving of the sociological definition, as also effected by the everyday discourse.

In research, the organisational definition is pushed forward within two fields of research, which have historically been distinct but which seem to fuse today. On the one hand is the sociology of professions (as described above) and on the other hand are the organisation studies. The first groups of studies show a tendency to focus on the interplay between professions and organisations from a professional perspective. By contrast, the second group of studies tend to approach the subject from an organisational perspective.

Studies of professions and organisations from a professional perspective[2]

Evetts (2003, 2011) has described some of the consequences of the fact that professionals increasingly work in large, global, and market-based organisations. Overall, she finds the terms 'profession' and 'professional' to be altered. Rather than attaining their meaning from the professions, the state, and central regulations, these words now attain meaning from organisational standards and targets. Furthermore, professional work is increasingly codified to fit contracts and evaluations made on the market. In other words, professional work is commodified. This includes relations to clients, who are now prone to be interpreted as customers (instead of clients).

Muzio and Kirckpatrick (2011) list a number of challenges, responses, and opportunities arising in the professions as a consequence of the organisational influence. Among the opportunities are so-called colonising tactics. They involve professions utilising the greater opportunities which appear in the organisations. In health, for example, 'doctors may take on management roles and acquire business qualifications . . . , in part, to buffer the practice of medicine against political and economic pressures of the environment' (Muzio & Kirckpatrick, 2011, p. 396). Among the challenges are new forms of re-stratification and professional projects that, in their attempt to accommodate new organisational demands, hollow out traditional notions of professionalism. Muzio and Kirckpatrick also mention an emerging body of research drawing on Foucauldian and poststructuralist perspectives. These studies focus on the 'hijacking' of professionalism to enhance and 'sneak in' corporate/organisational notions of professionalism (e.g. Fournier, 1999; Kipping, 2011) and on the consequent mediation, transformation, and re-creation of professional identities (Alvesson & Willmott, 2002; Hansen & Bøje, 2017; Karlsen & Villadsen, 2013; Waring & Currie, 2009). This happens through techniques such as performance appraisal, in-house training, mentoring, management by objectives, and even laughter.

Ackroyd et al. (2007) argue that new public management reforms in the UK have, in fact, not been very successful in changing professional values and institutions. This is especially the case in health care and social service, whereas housing seems to have been more open to change. They accord this to strategies of resistance among the professionals and to the reform process itself: due to their confrontational nature, reform processes have produced more opposition than would necessarily be the case had the politicians and leaders listened more to the professionals and their ideals of work.

In a Scandinavian context, Brante et al. (2015) have conducted a study on 17 professions across the public and private sector. Their conclusions are similar to those of Ackroyd et al., in that the professions are on defence and struggling to maintain their historic notions of professionalism. However, variances are found across the groups studied. Groups such as teachers, social workers, doctors, and nurses experience greater cuts and stronger management than groups such as economists, engineers, and architects (Brante et al., 2015, pp. 182–1092). In other words, professions carrying out public welfare services are more on defence than are private sector professions.

Hjort and Aili (2010) elaborate on the Scandinavian welfare workers. They describe a new competency among these professionals – what they call the ability to prioritise. This competency develops since welfare professionals must prioritise which master to follow: money, bureaucracy, or their own professional values.

Studies of professions and organisations from an organisational perspective

Scott (2008) studied the interplay between professions and organisations from an organisational perspective and, in a way, rediscovered the traits of the professions. He views them in continuation of his neo-institutional theory – a so-called pillar framework developed as a reaction to the widespread model of organisations as rational and market-driven. He describes the professions as 'the lords of the dance'; that is, as key agents for upholding the institutions of society. This description bears a striking resemblance to the descriptions made by Durkheim and Parsons decades ago. However, Scott also identifies changes and threats to the professions. These are similar to those described, for example, by Muzio and Kirckpatrick. He mentions a shift in the professional ethos where 'claimants to professional status have forsaken civic-minded moral appeals – "the social trusteeship" model that had long prevailed – to emphasise instead the value of "technical expertise", as validated by the market' (Scott, 2008, p. 232).

Noordegraaf (2011) argues that distinctions between professions and organisations and between professionals and managers are widely reproduced in research, even though they are problematic. His contribution is an attempt to overcome these distinctions, partly through the concept of organised professionalism. This concept assumes no contradiction between organisational and professional features: 'organising has been and will be an important dimension of professional work' (Noordegraaf, 2011, pp. 1357–1358). Furthermore, Noordegraaf observes research on the professions as normatively guided. This should explain the reproduction of the distinction between professions and organisations. However, Noordegraaf draws normative conclusions himself on how professionals and researchers studying the professions should proceed: they must learn to adapt to a new reality because not adapting is risky business. In this way, Noordegraaf describes and prescribes reality simultaneously.

The same applies to some Danish research on the so-called new professionals (Hein, 2009; Larsen & Hein, 2007). Here, the 'old' professionals are described in accordance with the critical branch of the sociology of professions – that is, as privileged groups who have been successful in using closure tactics to gain monopoly over restricted areas of work. At the same time, the 'new' professionals are prescribed through a range of imperatives: they must learn to cooperate with other occupations, accept bureaucratic control systems, learn how to zigzag in loosely coupled organisations, find balances between routine work and creative work, and get used to being managed.

Summary

The aim of this chapter was to provide a short review on professions, professionalism, and professionalisation to prepare and qualify the analyses and discussions in subsequent chapters. This alone may also qualify the current discourse and attempt to professionalise school leadership: what are we speaking of when we are speaking of this phenomenon?

We have reviewed a sociological and an organisational definition, both of which have been used in research on school leadership. The sociological definition is the earliest and most well-founded within research. We have traced it back to the works of Weber and Parsons and to the more recent neo-Weberians and trait analysis. The organisational definition has arisen in part because global organisations play an increasing role in framing and defining the work of professionals and in part because of the emptying and rephrasing of the sociological definition caused by everyday language. The organisational definition connects professions and professionalism to the standards and targets of market firms, rather than to the norms and values of individual professions, the state, laws, and regulations.

Viewed from the sociological definition, the current attempt to professionalise school leadership may seem futile. Many criteria must be accommodated, and school leadership is not the first occupation to have attempted this path – without clear success. Conversely, school leadership seems to be an emerging profession. In the following chapters, we will analyse and discuss to what extent and in what ways this may be the case.

Notes

1 Parsons' model case was medicine.
2 Parts resembling this section have previously been published in Hansen and Bøje (2017).

3 The knowledge base of school leadership

The development of a profession requires a certain stock of knowledge that enables the holders to perform their jobs and to separate them from those who do not hold that stock of knowledge. School leadership is not a traditional discipline with a long history. Conversely, it is also not a new field. It emerged together with many other practical sciences during the 18th and 19th centuries. The exact date of birth of the field is hard to determine, but the start might be a book written by Harold Payne in 1875 (Oplatka, 2010). As the history shows, the discipline does not follow a straight line from the origin to the present. The development is characterised by variation, change, interests, conflicts, and running attempts at demarcation vis-à-vis other disciplines and academic fields.

This development is important in the attempt to establish school leadership as a profession. What if no common and shared knowledge exists for school leaders to draw on when performing their work? What if, for instance, lawyers and doctors could choose between different lines of knowledge? Although variations and fluctuations might exist in the knowledge bases of these more established professions, we assume that they have a greater homogeneity compared to school leadership.

Setting the scene of the knowledge production in school leadership is the purpose of this chapter in the more comprehensive attempt to analyse professionalisation of school leadership. The initial step is to define what characterises a knowledge base. Here, we will rely on Andrew Abbott (1988), among others, and his synthetisation involving a so-called jurisdictional claim (cf. Chapter 2). Next, we present a historical sketch of the struggle to find and define a field. This sketch illustrates variations in perceptions and approaches to studies of school leadership, and, in so doing, it questions or relativises the premise of a knowledge base. Few (albeit, some) will claim school leadership to be a traditional scientific discipline. For one thing, the use and production of knowledge is not separated into distinct spheres (e.g. universities and schools) as with the division of labour seen in the

DOI: 10.4324/9781003033257-3

established professions. University researchers, consultants, and practitioners are all producers and consumers of knowledge – at the same time. The third step is to take a closer look at positions and approaches within the field, as unstable and varying as it may be. Among others, we describe the standards movement, which can be viewed as perhaps the most elaborate attempt to turn knowledge into behavioural standards and thereby professionalise school leadership. Fourth, we summarise and make a general assessment of the knowledge base in school leadership.

What is a knowledge base?

A knowledge base implies both practical and abstract forms of knowledge with which the professionals perform their work. Furthermore, this knowledge is both codified and embodied, laid down in textbooks, scientific journals, procedures, and institutions, and learned, used, and remembered by professionals in flesh and blood.

In the professions literature (cf. Chapter 2), the knowledge base is primarily associated with the abstract, codified, and textbook-like knowledge, although the practical and embodied form has also been given a fair amount of attention (e.g. Carlgren, 1990; Grimen & Molander, 2008; Schön, 1983). The functional approach to professions (cf. Chapter 2) generally views the knowledge base as synonymous with the breakthrough of the modern university, with science, rationalism, and progress, whereas the power approach attributes this knowledge to purposes of legitimation and social closure.

In a more balanced approach, Abbott (1988) describes academic knowledge as serving both purposes of legitimation and purposes of diagnosis, treatment, and inference. Furthermore, academic knowledge is vital to the so-called jurisdictional claim of professions, including emerging professions. Academic knowledge turns an objective field of work (e.g. the running of a school) into a subjective line of work (e.g. vision work, strategising, using assessment data to monitor student progress, etc.). Only through academic knowledge can a jurisdiction be defined, delineated vis-à-vis other professions and laymen, and maintained. The question is whether such a jurisdictional claim has been made by the alleged profession of school leadership. If so, through which forms of knowledge emanating from which fields of knowledge has this occurred?

Struggle for a field – a historical sketch

On the face of it, school leadership seems connected to almost indefinite fields of knowledge. The practice originates from teaching and from knowledge of children, pedagogy, didactics, curriculum, etc. Gradually, it has come to involve knowledge of economics, psychology, organisations, administration, sociology, philosophy, history, anthropology, data, statistics, and, more recently, research on leadership specifically. This is just to mention some areas from which a knowledge base can be constructed and, historically, has been attempted with varying degrees of success. On top of this come years of practical training and experience organised in more or less formal systems of education and recruitment.

As mentioned, the development of school leadership has not progressed linearly from the beginning till now. Rather, the route has been bumpy and dispersed, and this holds true for educational research as well. This situation has been subject to criticism, and some have argued that educational leadership, in a Kuhnian sense, is pre-paradigmatic and might be more properly structured in step with becoming more mature. Hargreaves (1996) comes close to stating this in his more general critique of educational research. According to him, educational research is too disperse and scattered, and everyone involved should instead decide to work in a more accumulative way on a shared and common project, striving for a better level of coherence. 'Educational research has failed to yield a corpus of research evidence that can be regarded as scientifically sound or as offering a worthwhile resource for guiding professional action' (Hargreaves, 1996, p. 4). If such a corpus were realised, a genuinely scientific field could emerge to the benefit and reputation of practice, according to Hargreaves.

However, school leadership was created to solve practical problems and was directed towards still more significant societal activities. To a large degree, the inspiration came from outside the school:

> As the function of the school has been enlarged in recent years, so that its conduct presents many new and complex problems, so new standards of efficiency must be recognised. It is interesting to study the organisation of a great commercial or industrial business and see what suggestion we may get to help us in the school.
> (Dutton, 1903; cited from English, 2002, p. 110)

Similar views occurred over the next decades, and a struggle arose for recognition in the university environment. It became crucial to be accepted as a science. In another extract from English (2002), in which he accounts for a book by Cubberley (1929), *Public School Administration*, first written in 1916, Cubberley is quoted as saying: 'His success as the head of a school system will to a rather large degree depend upon his intelligent understanding of the scientific and industrial world about him' (p. 224).

The endeavour to establish school leadership as a scientific field was closely related to Taylor's 'scientific management' as one of the first management theories. It laid out principles and hypotheses deduced from theory, which were then operationalised and tested empirically. For school leadership, having 'logical' administrative theories about decisions and behaviour was a breakthrough. In the late 1950s, this tradition was labelled 'the theory movement' (Culbertson, 1981; Greenfield, 1986; Gunter & Ribbins, 2003).

Commentators have noticed that leadership and accounts of leader behaviour became increasingly absent in this period. Until that point, a focus on historically great leaders (e.g. Gandhi and Churchill) were sources of inspiration. This approach was displaced by the attempt to establish school leadership as a scientific discipline. The contribution from psychology, which often is conceived as one of the main foundations of leadership, was also neglected. The main issues were those that could be calculated and prescribed.

The hegemony of the scientific approach decreased in the 1970s, with still more criticism coming from other positions in the humanities and social sciences (Greenfield & Ribbins, 1993). A broader palette of disciplines and approaches were allowed into the scene. English (2002) claims that, in this period, 'a point of scientificity' occurred with something like a boundary between inside and outside. This point of scientificity may be understood as a 'reverse Kuhn': from a kind of normal paradigm situation to an erosion. As English points out, 'there are no a priori meta-criteria to separate science from non-science in educational administration' (English, 2002, p. 109).

Attempts to define the field

This sketch shows that the struggle for establishing school leadership as a scientific discipline has not reached an end. Furthermore, it may not simply be a matter of maturity. A widespread view in the sociology of science is that researchers, although subscribing to shared scientific norms, constantly develop subfields and disciplines using a spectrum of scientific methods and a selective choice of their peers (Ziman, 1994).

A contribution which questions the possibility and appropriateness of scientific homogeneity is Burrell and Morgan's influential study on sociological paradigms in organisation studies (Burrell & Morgan, 1979). They used analyses of ontological and epistemological approaches to develop four paradigmatic lines that depend on whether researchers are realists or constructivists and have harmonic or critical perspectives. Several concepts in educational leadership have been subjected to studies using Burrell and Morgan's typology – for example, distributed leadership (Hartley, 2010).

Other contributions analysing obstacles to establish homogeneous fields of knowledge are Bourdieu (1988) and Whitley (2000). Both analyse the

The knowledge base of school leadership 25

cognitive and social dimensions of the struggle for positioning and in the academic field. Whitley notes that, especially for practice-oriented disciplines such as school leadership, recognition from groups outside academia (e.g. politicians and corporate leaders) has great importance.

Gunter and Ribbins (2003) have attempted to map the field of research on educational leadership by studying *processes, positions, producers, practices*, and *perspectives*. Through this, they have identified a number of positions, called *conceptual, descriptive, humanistic, critical, evaluative*, and *instrumental*. These positions have later been elaborated by Gunter and Forrester (2009), who reported a study on knowledge production in educational leadership. Their study draws close attention to the connections that exist between school leadership as an occupation and the political and economic actors that influence this occupation – specifically, New Labour and the National College for School Leadership (NCSL). Using Bourdieu and Foucault as theoretical inspiration, three *regimes of practice* are identified as currently representing the state of British educational leadership. These regimes are depicted in the model in Figure 3.1, adopted from Gunter and Forrester's work.

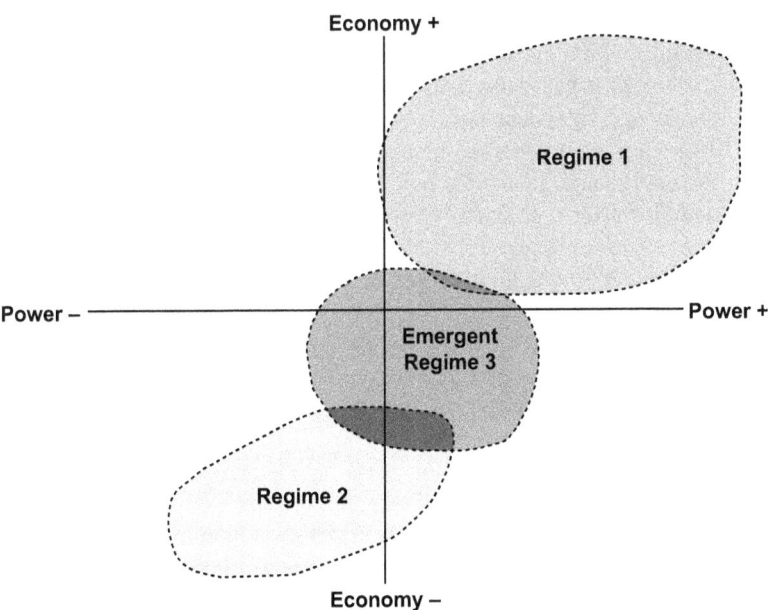

Figure 3.1 Regimes of practice under New Labour
Source: Gunter & Forrester (2009, p. 503)

Regime 1 is based on political as well as economic power (+ on the horizontal and vertical axes). According to Gunter and Forrester, this regime is currently the dominating one. Those positioned in this regime tend to be *ministers* appointed by the prime minister; *civil servants* 'moving around within and between departments'; *advisors* from local government, universities, business, and schools; and *consultants* from universities and private-sector companies.

Short of political and economic power, regime 2 is currently the dominated position. Those occupying this position 'are mainly in universities, are researchers and are leading members of their fields with national and international reputations' (Gunter & Forrester, 2009, p. 505). Furthermore, regime 2 occupants tend to:

- Problematise the historical legacy of leader-centric structures and cultures
- Locate employment in higher education institutions and frame their work as research
- Emphasise how neo-liberal agendas dominate, at the expense of narratives about democratic development and social justice
- Use social theories regarding class and gender, and draw on theories of power, such as those of Foucault and Bourdieu, to frame investigations
- Identify with a discipline with a tendency to be sociologists and/or to be located in the wider area of public policy where they are not just concerned with education
- Use reflexive approaches to their own and others' roles in knowledge production and debate the relationship between power, the economy, and professional practice

To some extent, this depicts regime 2 members as the 'good guys', while regime 1 members are depicted the 'bad guys'. At least this is the impression one might get when reading this description from an outside, Scandinavian position. We will return to this observation in Chapter 4 and use it as one of the means to navigate the (sub)field of school leader education and preparation.

Regime 3 is described as an emergent regime attracting members 'from the fringes of Regimes 1 and 2' (Gunter & Forrester, 2009, p. 506). It *could* be constituted by practitioners interested in the power structures influencing their everyday lives, and, vice versa, those in power interested in the everyday lives of teachers, students, parents, etc. However, according to Gunter and Forrester, there is currently

> more interest in positioning in relation to Regimes 1 and 2 than in creating another regime. For a third regime to emerge there would need

to be a direct linkage between those in higher education and in schools who want to generate alternative strategies to that which currently dominate through Regime 1 practices.

(Gunter & Forrester, 2009, pp. 506–507)

Positions and approaches within the field

Until now, we have focussed on ways to historicise and define what could be a knowledge base of school leadership. In the following, we look more deeply into positions and approaches within the field, as unstable and varying as it may be.

From managerial to transformational, interpretive, and instructional leadership

In an overview article, Harris (2005) attempts to distinguish four approaches to leadership, including the theoretical underpinnings of these and their connection to broader schemes of organisation. She uses a typology developed by Bush and Glover (2003), who used a typology developed by Leithwood et al. (1999). On this basis, Harris distinguishes between:

- Managerial forms of leadership – in short, management
- Transformational leadership
- Instructional leadership
- Interpretive leadership

These four approaches are not mutually exclusive. The first, which is managerial or transactional, is described by Harris as a rational form of leadership rooted in scientific management theories and the total quality management movement. It was dominant until the 1980s. Its focus is on structures and rules, and it is associated with bureaucracy, technical rationalism, goal fixation, structure, and management of systems and processes rather than people and action. Furthermore, 'this form of leadership equates leadership with a series of transactions within an organisation and has been termed "transactional leadership"' (Harris, 2005, p. 78). Harris also finds 'the systems management approaches within the National Qualification for Headteachers (NPQH) [to] reflect certain aspects of transactional leadership' (Harris, 2005, p. 78). This approach is no longer dominant, but it remains an important bedrock for school leadership within a steering chain of accountability and responsibility.

In opposition to the former approach, transformational leadership is described as a later and more promising form of leadership. It was originally developed by Burns (1978) and Bass (1990), with a focus on relations rather than structures. Theoretically, it is associated with the development of shared goals, intrinsic motivation, and the concept of culture, although exactly how and to what extent is not clear. The key idea is the transformational leader who develops an organisation culture in which everyone – leaders, as well as followers – share a common goal. In this sense, transformational leadership is about change: change of culture and change of organisation, typically with a purpose of improving student performance. Furthermore, transformational leadership is described as moral art rather than technical science. Therefore, it includes 'charisma, inspirational motivation, intellectual stimulation and individualised consideration' (Harris, 2005, p. 79). Lastly, Harris, via Leithwood, connects transformational leadership to school improvement, involving both teachers' motivation and collaboration and student performance, and this seems to be one of the reasons for the impact of this approach on educational leadership. Apparently, transformational leadership is both the 'right' thing to do and an 'effective' means of doing it. Notably, transformational leadership, in the words of Leithwood, shapes behaviours (not actions) that 'have been shown to encourage teacher collaboration, to increase teacher motivation and to improve teachers' self-efficacy' (Harris, 2005, p. 80).

Some attempts to measure transformational leadership have been developed. Leithwood et al. (1999) have established a framework focussing on four main categories, namely (1) setting directions, (2) helping people, (3) redesigning the organisation, and (4) the transactional and managerial aggregate. The focus on the effects of the leader, and, in some instances, charismatic leadership (e.g. Hinkin & Tracey, 1999; House, 1976), is closely related to a stream of literature (e.g. Clark & Salaman, 1996; Collins, 2005) in which leaders are perceived, analysed, and, in some cases, treated as gurus with almost supernatural skills.

Critics of transformational and charismatic leadership (e.g. Yukl, 1999) address the underlying processes of influence, which remain unclear. Another point is the emphasis on dyadic relations between individuals, which may lead to neglect of collaboration and other group-related processes.

Interpretive leadership is more specifically discussed as distributed leadership, with reference to Gronn (2003) and Spillane et al. (2001) in particular. The theoretical root of this type of leadership is claimed to be Engeström's activity theory where 'the notion of activity bridges the gap between agency and structure' (Harris, 2005, p. 81). Distributed leadership attempts to adjust former theories of hierarchy and bureaucracy, stressing leadership as essentially a distributed activity performed by many leaders of an organisation – formal as well as informal and top leaders as well as middle managers and even teachers and other professionals. Furthermore, distributed leadership is described as an analytical perspective, not a prescriptive or normative perspective. This also seems so in the case of Gronn (2003) and Spillane et al. (2001), whereas in Harris' case, it is more questionable. Again, she connects distributed leadership to evidence and effect, stating 'despite the widespread and growing enthusiasm for distributed leadership within the educational research community, specific empirical evidence about the phenomenon is less forthcoming' (Harris, 2005, p. 82). In doing this, she seems to evaluate distributed leadership from a normative and utilitarian point of view.

Lastly, instructional leadership is formulated with reference to a discourse of improvement, evidence, and effectiveness. Theoretical underpinnings are rather absent, although some mention is made of agency and leadership 'as focusing upon the relationships among people hence crossing organisational boundaries' (Harris, 2005, p. 82); however, the description remains short and vague. In return, attention is given to more normatively guided ideas and propositions. Among these is a distinction between 'narrow' and 'broad' instructional leadership. Narrow instructional leadership focusses on actions directly related to teaching and learning, whereas the broader conception includes administration, school culture, and other variables indirectly influencing instruction and learning. The broader conception also involves ideas and norms of capacity building and human capital investment. This broader conception is sometimes referred to as 'pedagogical leadership' (Male & Palaiologou, 2012).

Hallinger (2005), one of the main proponents of instructional leadership, presents his contribution as a model and a framework. This model or framework consists of several functions, with (1) defining the school's mission, (2) managing the instructional program, and (3) promoting a positive school learning climate as the main ones. With this framework, Hallinger points out that instructional leadership has much in common with transformational leadership and is as instrumental as critics have argued.

An offshoot of this approach can be found in Robinson's student-centred leadership (Robinson, 2011). Through meta-analysis of several studies, she tries to determine which factors, referred to as *effect sizes*, affect student learning and how leaders might lead according to the most important of these factors.

Standards, standards, standards

Another important contribution to the field is the current attempt to construct standards – in the USA and the UK first and foremost. In Denmark and other Scandinavian countries, we have not moved as far in this direction, although the tendency is discernible. These standards comprise abstract as well as practical and embodied forms of knowledge.

Murphy (2005), a chief protagonist and developer of standards in the USA, has described the historic background of the standards of the Interstate School Leaders Licensure Consortium (ISLLC). In his account, the development of standards formed part of a more general attempt to 're-culture' the so-called profession of school leadership. Notably, in Murphy's account, school leadership is referred to unambiguously as a profession. From this point of view, an attempt to analyse and discuss school leadership as an emerging profession may seem futile.

In any case, the re-culturing of the profession is supposed to have happened through a deconstruction and dismissal of the previous content and disciplines involved in the practice of school leadership and the training and education of school leaders. Murphy mentions these disciplines or 'knowledge blocks' as (1) business management and (2) behavioural and social sciences. Business management, or the adoption of ideas and practices from the private sector, dominated in the beginning of the 20th century until the Second World War, when the behavioural and social sciences became dominant. Together, these disciplines constituted a 'two-layered foundation built up during the 19th century' (Murphy, 2005, p. 156).[1] Around the 1990s, however, Murphy and the rest of the ISLLC, which includes researchers, consultants, practitioners, and, to some (but an unspecified) extent, politicians, decided 'not to focus on the two questions that had guided the development of the field for the past century: (a) What is afoot in the corporate world that we can borrow to rethink the work of school leaders? and (b) What is unfolding in the behavioural sciences that can be applied to power reform efforts?' (Murphy, 2005, p. 158). Rather, they raised a series of eight questions and developed groups to discuss these to propose a new framework on which the profession of school leadership could be founded. The result of this work is the now ten standards (originally six) which frame the work of school leaders, structure their education and training, and form a basis for systems of licensure and accreditation (National Policy Board for Educational Administration, 2015).

The knowledge behind these standards can be described as, on the one hand, a learning discourse focussing on evidence-based connections between administration and student achievement and, on the other hand, a moral discourse voiced on behalf of coloured and socially disadvantaged children. The learning discourse, in a way, redirects leadership and administration to what is said to be the core purpose of schools – namely, teaching and learning, but in a manner where evidence and effectiveness play key roles. Omitted is the previous two-layered foundation consisting of business management and the behavioural and social sciences. The learning discourse and the moral discourse are often mixed and presented in an aggregative way, suggesting that standards improve schools for all (as measured by grades) *and* take care of poor children. For example:

> So too, the spotlight in this literature is clearly directed at youngsters who had been left behind in America's schools for nearly a century, especially children from low-income homes, students of colour, and pupils with a first language other than English.
> (Murphy, 2005, pp. 159–160)

That the two aims may conflict – for instance, if a school leader must choose between enrolling academically able students who can normally raise the numbers or socially disadvantaged children – is never discussed. The idea seems to be that standards fit all.

However, Murphy and the standards movement have received criticism in the academic field. We focus here on English (2000, 2006) and Gronn (2002), as they have put forward arguments that are most relevant to our purpose – the discussion of a knowledge base of school leadership.

In an early commentary, English (2000) compared the standards project to a religion. Provokingly, he titles the commentary *Pssssst! What does one call a set of non-empirical beliefs required to be accepted on faith and enforced by authority? [Answer: a religion, aka the ISLLC standards]*. According to English, the standards are *not* empirically based (i.e. developed through empirical, analytic, and scholarly work) but are instead derived through normatively guided questions, hopes, expectations, and promises retrospectively couched in articulations of evidence, effect, and improvement. In other words, they express ingredients of a secular religion (on this subject, see also Bøje, 2020). In a later and academically sounder article, English (2006) extends his criticism. The most important arguments are:

- From a postmodern view, which English takes up, there can be no knowledge base. Any attempt to construct such is more damaging than constructive. The current attempt, expressed in modernistic and positivist notions such as 'pillars', 'foundations', 'core technology', 'ISLLC architecture', and so on, stifles the field rather than contributes to its dynamic. Thus, English prefers to speak of a knowledge dynamic instead of a knowledge base.
- The standards are ahistorical, inflexible, and impossible to use as part of a reflective practice of school leadership. In English's words,

> the standards represent disembodied skills, concepts, and ideas distanced from the theories that spawned them. They are in and

of themselves ahistorical, the result of which is that they possess no internal cohesion. There is no overall conceptual scheme to unite them.

(English, 2006, p. 463)

- An unintended consequence of the standards is in fact a lowering of standards and ultimately a deprofessionalisation of the occupation. This happens not least because the licensure and accreditation system associated with the standards limits the universities from the provision of education and training. Instead, cheaper, more short-term, and market-oriented 'alternatives' take over.

In his article from 2005, Murphy attempts to accommodate some of the critique. On the second argument – that the standards are too rigid and untheoretical – Murphy makes the counterargument that some critics find the standards too concrete (such as English), while others find them too vague and lacking in specificity. How can they be both at the same time? According to Murphy, this contradiction shows the internal flaws of the critics: they are more preoccupied with paradigmatic struggle and positioning than with moving forward. This is an argument similar to that of Hargreaves (1996).

In our reading, the standards are, in fact, both too concrete and too abstract at the same time – not possible to think with and too generic to use in specific contexts vis-à-vis concrete schools, teachers, children, etc. This makes the standards all-embracing and potentially hegemonic, a point also made by English.

Gronn (2002) adds to the discussion by developing a notion of designer leadership. Designer leadership is characterised by an active and politically motivated attempt to 'produce individuals fit for leadership roles and to guarantee the production of successive requisite cohorts of institutional-level leaders' (Gronn, 2002, p. 557). Gronn contrasts this mode of leadership production to former ways of being or becoming a leader: first, by *ascription*, entailing a set of elite, heredity, and aristocratic selection criteria. Here, the leader is born to be a leader. Second, by *achievement* entailing a set of meritocratic selection criteria developed and governed within institutions of higher education. Here, the leader has qualified to become a leader. The distinctive feature of designer leadership is the technological production of leaders through standards institutionalised in 'a regime of compliance and an industry of verification' (Gronn, 2002, p. 556).

Gronn also distinguishes between the standards movement in the USA and the UK. In the USA, the project was formed by 'a broad coalition of stakeholders anchored on the NPBEA' (Gronn, 2002, p. 562) or, in Murphy's terms, a consortium. These stakeholders have gradually co-opted other national bodies, such as the Council of Chief State School Officers (CCSSO), to impose standards on the majority of states, universities, and other providers of teacher and leader training programmes. In the UK, the invention and imposition of standards is supposed to have happened in a more top-down political fashion. In Gronn's words:

> If the solution, proffered by the British prime minister Tony Blair, for the attainment of a world-competitive British economy, following the accession to office of the Labour government in May 1997, was said to be "Education, education, education," now "Standards, standards, standards" has become the mantra of school reformers.
> (Gronn, 2002, p. 553)

In both cases, however, standards constitute an overwhelming factor in the general practice of school leadership and in the knowledge base specifically.

Danish and Scandinavian contributions

In Denmark, the effort to develop a common knowledge base of school leadership is modest. There is not much research to constitute this base, and, compared to teaching, nursing, and social work, for example, the stakes are (still) small. In the education and training programmes, the knowledge taught is international and has a 'borrowed' nature in that it originates from business management, organisation theory, philosophy, and the social and behavioural sciences. This is similar to the situation described by Murphy in the USA before the ISLLC standards. School leaders have practical experience, but this experience is not well studied, codified, and ordered into something that resembles a knowledge base. Mostly, it is expressed as normative expectations of what school leaders *should* be doing as high hopes, wishes, visions, and codes of behaviour (e.g. Lederforeningen, 2008; Væksthus for Ledelse, 2008).

Lejf Moos, a longtime researcher and developer of school leadership in Denmark, describes the state of the art as follows:

> The politically motivated gap – and competition – between universities and university colleges has had serious repercussions on research. There are clear indications that researchers research in subjects that their institutions teach. Therefore, most of the research on leadership, done by the university colleges' researchers, is on generic, public leadership, while only a few researchers from universities investigate on specific school leadership, principals' work, values and reflections.
> (Moos, 2016, p. 18)

In his own research, Moos focusses on shifts in the overall governance of the public sector – from universal Welfarism to New Public Management and competition – and the consequences these may have to school leadership. Furthermore, he has made in-depth qualitative studies describing the practices and everyday life of school leaders (Moos et al., 2000; 2011). In this way, he has shed light on the otherwise unknown stock of practical experience used in the practice of school leadership.

Other research has produced the genealogy of leadership in the Danish public sector (Rennisson, 2006), conditions of middle management across public sector institutions (Klausen et al., 2011), ideas of psy-leadership (Staunæs et al., 2009), coupling of institutional organisation theory and school leaders' perceptions of organisational change (Raae, 2008), paradoxes and tensions in management of professionals (teachers) in upper secondary school (Jacobsen & Buch, 2016), discursive connections between school leadership literature and practice (Hansen & Frederiksen, 2017), experiences of practically oriented training programmes (Hjort et al., 2018), and effects of school leadership on the implementation of primary and lower secondary school reform (Winter, 2017). As interesting and valuable as this may be, it is not what is usually associated with academic knowledge in the professions literature. For example, in medicine, Abbott (1988, p. 53) uses examples such as etiology, gross pathology, and micropathology. In law, examples are rights, duties, and procedures. These knowledge areas are 'dictated by its custodians, the academics, whose criteria are not practical clarity and efficacy, but logical consistency and rationality' (Abbott, 1988, p. 53). Even if comparing school leadership to medicine and law seems unfair, these examples may indicate the current status of the Danish – and possibly the global – knowledge base of school leadership. The clear division of labour between academics and practitioners in the established professions is notable, but the same does not apply to school leadership.

In Norway and Sweden, Ärlestig et al. (2016), Møller (2016), Nihlfors and Johansson (2013), and Uljens and Ylimaki (2017) are some of the prominent researchers and developers. Ottesen (2016) has made an interesting and explicit attempt to analyse the Nordic knowledge base of school leadership, suggesting it is scattered and insecure and that its future may be rooted in pedagogy, which is an older discipline established prior to notions of learning, evidence, effect, and improvement. Furthermore, she argues discretion (in Abbott's terms: inference) should be given stronger attention, as this is a key aspect of professional work. Grimen and Molander (2008) have argued no need exists for professions and professionals if no indeterminacy exists – hence, the use of discretion in this line of work. If actions and procedures are completely explained and laid out in ready scripts or standards, work takes the form of an industrial assembly line to the detriment of the client who expects individual treatment. It may be this scenario that English, Gronn, and others dread when assessing the standards movement in the USA and the UK. We will return to the question of discretion in Chapter 6.

A knowledge base of school leadership?

The remaining question is whether the above described knowledge, positions, fields, and approaches can meaningfully be summarised as a knowledge base of school leadership. The answer to this question depends, of course, on the definition of a knowledge base. Here, as a first step, we have relied on Abbott (1988) and his sociological definition, in which academic knowledge is the decisive factor. This knowledge must be abstract, but not too abstract, and codified for purposes of diagnosis, treatment, and inference. Furthermore, abstract knowledge is vital to jurisdictional claims – that is, demarcation and delineation vis-à-vis other professions and laymen.

Whether the knowledge produced and used in relation to school leadership qualifies for this definition remains in question. Historically, attempts have been made to raise a science of school leadership in the shape of the theory movement, but these attempts diminished sometime later. Hargreaves (1996) laments this in his more general critique of educational research, arguing for more coherence, accumulation of knowledge, and collaboration towards shared goals. Similarly, the standards movement can be seen as an attempt to unify the alleged profession around hard evidence, studies of effectiveness, and standards expressing true knowledge. However, standards also standardise and exclude knowledge and actors, and this has resulted in criticism from various actors. Therefore, the standards movement may be another futile attempt to raise a science of school leadership.

Why do these attempts discontinue? Several reasons may explain this, but one has to do with the practical nature characterising school leadership. It is (also) a practice performed by people in everyday contexts, and this opens it up to personal experiences, opinions, values, norms, good advice, gurus, etc. Political and economic pressures also arise. Thus, scientific aspiration is constantly challenged by practical experience.

This may also apply to the classic professions – theology, medicine, law, and engineering – which form a base for Abbott's definition and the sociology of professions in general. Abbott's definition is that abstract knowledge is *also* used for purposes of legitimation. This means that abstract knowledge may not, first and foremost, have a functional role even in the established professions; rather, it serves a legitimising and power reproducing role. The established professions and, to some extent, the sociology of professions (especially the friendly branch) as their auxiliary arm may simply be better at telling a tale about themselves and their reliance on abstract knowledge.

Another reason for the difficulties in becoming a science and, consequently, establishing a knowledge base as defined by Abbott is the fact that the production of knowledge takes place in a field with competing positions and actors. A lot is at stake in this 'battlefield', and this makes believing in consensus, collaboration, accumulation of knowledge, and shared goals naïve if not hegemonic. As pointed out by Gunter and Forrester (2009), at least three regimes of practice can be identified in a struggle to define school leadership: (1) a dominant regime close to political and economic power, (2) a dominated and intellectual regime short of political and economic power, and (3) an emergent regime attracting members from the fringes of regimes 1 and 2.

This competition is not necessarily a drawback to the ambition of becoming a profession. According to English (2006), a knowledge dynamic, rather than a knowledge base, is preferred. The concept of a knowledge dynamic respects contestation of knowledge, and it allows practitioners to be the reflexive users and co-producers of knowledge. As such, the concept may come closer to stating how knowledge is actually produced and used in school leadership, as well as in the established professions.

Note

1 We believe Murphy means the 20th century here.

4 Education and preparation of school leaders

The education and preparation of school leaders vary within and among countries, despite apparent similarities and incipient global patterns. In the USA and the UK, the majority of programmes are directed at aspiring K–12 leaders without experience, whereas programmes in Denmark and other Nordic countries, due to our history and context, are directed at experienced leaders. In most countries, formal education does not have a long history; the United States was a front-runner in establishing education and organisations providing school leadership education.

The increasing belief in the importance of school leaders in the performance of schools and students has resulted in a corresponding interest and attempt to study school leadership education, assuming this to be a contributing variable to school leadership as a general and aggregate variable. The amount of literature on this subject is astonishing. Compared with other subjects covered in this book, education is by far the most researched subject. Within the dominant positions, the questions and issues raised are typically these:

- How important (effective) is school leader education?
- What are the mediating circumstances (e.g. states, universities, and local school conditions)?
- How can it be measured?
- How can effectiveness be attained through formulation and implementation of standards – in the education programmes and in the systems of licensure and accreditation?
- What are the gaps in the knowledge base of leadership education?
- How can theory and practice be bridged?

Among the critics, the questions and issues raised include:

- What good do standards do if the problem is the standard of the candidates enrolled in these programmes?

DOI: 10.4324/9781003033257-4

- What is the purpose of nationalising and standardising the market of educational provision through the imposition of standards?
- How is education related to identity formation?
- Does education of school leaders fulfil the purposes we want it to – and does it resemble the education we want for our children?

In this chapter, we analyse and discuss the status of school leader education and preparation – internationally and in the Nordic context – with an aim of assessing how this contributes to the current attempt to professionalise school leadership. First, we describe the international context, focussing on literature which covers both dominant and marginal positions, so-called orthodoxies and heterodoxies. As in the previous chapter, we do not claim to make a comprehensive review of the field. These reviews already exist, and our purpose here is to focus on the issue of professionalisation. Next, we describe some Danish cases that exemplify key issues and concerns to school leadership education in a post-welfare state, which is a context undergoing modernisation and globalisation. We end by summing up and addressing the central question of professionalisation of school leadership.

The international context

Many of the endeavours in the international context are aimed at identifying the optimal school leader education. Literature and research seek to 'fill the gaps' between what we know and what we need to know to attain the preferred educational system. A shared hope in many settings seems to be that filling these gaps can 'help the field reach a consensus about preparing leaders for the current policy context' (Hallinger, 2013; cited in Crow & Whiteman, 2016). Few will doubt that research influences the supply of education, but many will doubt that, on this basis, the shared community can create the single best education.

Orthodoxies

From the many variations of education and training programmes for school leaders, we present, in the following, some of the most influential topics which have been discussed in the declared hope of finding a more optimal design for school leader education. We regard these topics and the ones discussing them as constituting the dominant positions or orthodoxies within the field. Against them, the critics or heterodoxies raise questions and focus on other topics relevant to school leader education.

We elaborate on the heterodoxies below. At this point, however, the homology is worth noting between the division of positions in the educational field and the division of positions in the knowledge base, as described in the previous chapter. Identifying intermediary positions is possible, as suggested by Gunter and Forrester (2009) in their study (represented as an emergent regime 3), and we try to maintain attention on these.

Filling the gaps and improving school leader education

In a study commissioned by the American University Council for Educational Administration (UCEA) and the Wallace Foundation, Crow and Whiteman (2016) attempted to map the research base of educational leadership preparation programmes. They began with the 2009 handbook by Young et al. (2009) and established their list of programme features, which included context, candidates, faculty, curriculum, design, delivery, pedagogy, internships, student assessment, mentoring and coaching, comprehensive leadership development, and programme evaluation. From there, they attempted to expose what has happened – and what has not happened – in a four-year period up to 2013. Their research interest is in 'knowing the extent to which the research base on programme features has developed since 2009, including ways in which the literature has or has not addressed questions or gaps identified in the *Handbook*' (Crow & Whiteman, 2016, p. 121). They also believe 'a review of the research base can help the field reach a consensus about preparing school leaders for the current policy context' (p. 120) even if consensus is not always necessary. Consensus may result in blindness to the local needs of schools, according to Crow and Whiteman.

They find the (American) knowledge base of preparation programmes to have expanded and evolved in the studied period. They believe more is known about the features that should be included for the programmes to be effective. A study by Darling-Hammond et al. (2010) is mentioned in particular and taken more or less as a blueprint for the design of effective education programmes. That study presents the following programme features as key to effectiveness:

- Rigorous recruitment and selection
- Research-based content
- Curricular coherence
- Field-based internships
- Problem-based learning strategies
- Cohort structures
- Mentoring or coaching
- Collaboration between universities and school districts

In addition to this finding, Crow and Whiteman identify some still existing gaps in the knowledge base. These are methodological and ontological or field-focussed. Methodologically, Crow and Whiteman deplore the predominance of descriptive studies and point to the need for more effect studies, longitudinal studies (that show how candidates' knowledge, skills, and dispositions develop over time), and cross-institutional comparisons. In terms of field knowledge, more knowledge is needed regarding the background of the candidates and the ways in which they are recruited. Lastly, they find that continuous leadership development is an under-explored theme.

Interestingly, the review does not speak much about standards for education programmes. There is some mention of it, but not to the extent suggested by the proponents of standards. The review also does not include providers other than universities, since 'the large majority of educational leaders are still trained in university programmes and by far the largest focus of research is on these programmes' (p. 122). Had the review focussed more on standards, it would perhaps have included alternative providers permitted through standards-driven systems of accreditation. This omission may be interpreted as a subtle criticism of the standards movement that, in turn, provides grounds for assigning Crow and Whiteman an intermediary field position, as referred to above.

The (great) importance of education and preparation

Throughout the field (that is, among the orthodoxies and, to a lesser extent, the heterodoxies), an established truth – a doxa – seems to be that school leadership education is important for or has an effect on the practice of school leadership, which in turn is important for or has an effect on the performance of schools and students. The question is not whether this is in fact true, but rather to what extent and in some cases how/why it is so. Thus, the rather long causal chain from education – practice – school – teachers – students' grades is more or less taken for granted. If it is discussed, it is merely in terms of what 'mediating circumstances' and/or 'confounding variables' might obstruct the importance of education.

In the now many and rather extensive handbooks on educational leadership preparation and education, this recognition or acknowledgement of the importance of education is expressed in some recurrent and common sense-like phrases. Just to take one example, Lumby et al. (2008) state: 'We believe the rationale for such a volume is strong and is based on the evolving recognition of both the importance of leadership, and leadership development and preparation' (p. 1). And: 'Reports and articles, primarily in the UK, Australia, New Zealand, Sweden, Canada, and the US, have acknowledged the importance of understanding how school leaders prepare for and develop their roles' (p. 3). Lastly: 'The acknowledgement of the importance of preparation and development has not always been followed by rigorous empirical research' (p. 3). Here, 'recognition' and 'acknowledgement' of the importance of school leadership education is repeated. In Young et al. (2009), with a more US focus, the perspective is to gather a deeper empirical foundation in an attempt to respond to criticisms raised against many existing preparation programmes. Current and upcoming leaders declare they cannot use their educational merits and they do not feel prepared for the actual challenges in schools.

Pounder (2011),[1] in a special issue on leader preparation in *Education Administration Quarterly*, summarises the latest findings on the effect of school leader education programmes – as these are described in the other articles included in this special journal issue. Generally, these studies employ a quantitative and 'outcome-oriented evaluative approach' (p. 260), through which attempts are made to analyse statistic correlations between programme types and programme features on the one hand and grades and other measures among candidates on the other hand. Going a step further in the causal chain, some studies attempt to find correlations between programmes and programme features on the one hand and 'the development of well-qualified teacher teams in schools' (p. 261) on the other hand. Furthermore, relations between teacher-team quality (as somehow measured) and student achievement are analysed in the last instance, thereby covering the entire causal chain from education programme to student effect. Similarly, a study by Orr and Orphanos (2011) is highlighted for 'directly [comparing] leadership practices of 125 principals who completed one of four "exemplary" leadership preparation programmes compared with a national sample of more than 500 principals from "conventional" preparation programs' (p. 261). In the next step, these two groups of principals are compared on the level of school improvement, as measured by the extent to which they engage in effective instructional and organisational leadership practices (not student achievement).

These examples show how this group of orthodoxies is preoccupied with measuring the effect of school leader education – not questioning or explaining it. As such, the long causal chain covered (and acknowledged) by these studies remains largely a black box. It should be recognised, however, that caution and reflection are expressed at the end of Pounder's article. For example, she discusses the relations between quality leadership and education, as measured in the mentioned studies, and the socioeconomics and resources at the studied schools by asking whether the higher measures of quality at some schools are in fact measures of socioeconomics, resources, and family privilege. Quality measures are certainly positively correlated with family resources: the higher the schools score on quality measures, the higher the resources are among families. Furthermore, she discusses if this significance of resources obscures the suggested causality between high-quality education and high-quality leadership practice: do some leaders at resourced schools practice high-quality leadership not because of prior education experience but because it is easier and in fact expected at these schools? Put more boldly: do leaders lead schools or do schools (also) lead leaders?

Standards in education and training

As opposed to Crow and Whiteman (2016), Pounder (2011) emphasises the role of standards in the education and preparation of school leaders. She refers to one study by Roach et al. (2011) which shows that:

> the Interstate School Leader Licensure Consortium standards (and resultant Educational Leadership Constituent Council standards) have had perhaps the greatest impact on state administrator quality policy, with these standards infused in preparation program standards, candidate assessment and licensure, program approval or accreditation, and graduate mentoring and induction.
>
> (Pounder, 2011, p. 259)

Reading the US blueprint, the National Educational Leadership Preparation (NELP) Program Recognition Standards (National Policy Board for Educational Administration, 2018), which is an extension and elaboration of the original work performed by the Interstate School Leaders Licensure Consortium (ISLLC standard, see Chapter 3) standards, the same conclusion comes to mind. Generally, the paper gives the impression that the eight suggested standards[2] now permeate every aspect of school leader education in the USA. This is a different picture than the one given by Crow and Whiteman (2016), raising the possibility that the proponents of standards – the standards movement – overestimate the significance and spread of these compared with what happens at the ground floor level – that is, at the universities. Still, assessing to what extent standards dominate the provision of school leader education in the USA and in the UK is impossible. We can merely observe their presence and role among the orthodoxies, which is dissimilar to the case in Denmark and other Nordic countries.

Theory and practice

A fourth theme concerns the relation between theory and practice in education programmes. Even if the orthodoxies generally express aims of bridging theory and practice as one way of improving school leadership, the relation between the two entities is often presented as a crude dichotomy: either you are with theory or you are with practice. At other times, the relation is described as a one-dimensional continuum: the closer one is to one pole, the greater the distance to the other. Moreover, the relation between theory and practice is expressed in a number of overlapping yet slightly different terms – for example, technical-rational knowledge and artistry, experiential and academic learning, generic and context-specific skills (Schön, 1987; cited in McCarthy & Forsyth, 2009, p. 86).

These tensions appear in the distinction between formal and informal education. In formal education, especially at the universities, the emphasis is on theoretical knowledge, whereas in informal education, the focus is on practice and experiential knowledge and learning. Zhang and Brundrett (2010) report a study where school leaders prefer experiential learning rather than academic knowledge presented in formal courses. One of the main explanations is that it may provide better opportunities for school leaders to manage the next day's tasks.

Among orthodoxies, the general idea seems to be that theory and academic knowledge and learning are too abstract and distant. Similar considerations have existed for a long time in general leadership education – for example, in business schools or MBA programmes (Augier & March, 2011). One of the main questions has always been whether one can learn in school or university to become a leader, or whether this is primarily a personal attribute developed through experience. Mintzberg (2011) has argued leadership is not a profession but an art regulated by the market.

The tension between theory and practice became obvious in the preparation of a new reform of Danish primary school leader education (Kommunernes Landsforening, 2017). The reform committee, which consisted of nine members (of which only one represented Danish schools), prepared a proposal for a new common education for all leaders in the Danish primary school. They referred to a trend wherein the education during the last ten years had become more practice-oriented, and they argued this should continue to an even more practice-oriented profile. They did not present any evidence of the usefulness of this profile, but still 'the committee emphasises the need of a swift transition to a new and more practical training of school leaders' (Kommunernes Landsforening, 2017, p. 4, our translation). Besides the emphasis on less theory and more practice, the importance of an immediate and instrumental use of education is stressed: 'School leaders should therefore have competencies and effective leadership tools that can be immediately applied in the everyday life of schools' (Kommunernes Landsforening, 2017, p. 9, our translation).

This reform proposal has triggered a response from a well-known Danish leadership researcher (Hildebrandt, 2017). Besides noticing a lack of conceptual clarity and methodological precision, he points out the inappropriateness of a single education for all school leaders: 'I would warn against designing a leadership education for all leaders in the Danish primary and lower secondary school – and I would especially warn against doing so based on what the current school leaders think is right' (Hildebrandt, 2017, p. 29, our translation).

Heterodoxies

A large amount of time and effort is invested by the heterodoxies to criticise or comment on the works and ideas of the orthodoxies. This seems to express the power relations existing between the two groups: the orthodoxies set the agenda, while the heterodoxies are busy making comments on the direction chosen. Thus, the heterodoxies can encounter difficulties in presenting their own ideas and visions of school leadership (education).

Still, both groups seem to share the illusion that the struggle is worth fighting. Both groups make investments in the field and attempt to accrue capital (cultural, material, or symbolic). These investments take the form of positionings or stances based on the actors' positions within the field. As explained by Bourdieu:

> it is not, as is usually thought, political stances which determine people's stances on things academic, but their positions in the academic field which inform the stances that they adopt on political issues in general as well as on academic problems.
>
> (Bourdieu, 1988, pp. xvii–xviii)

In the case of the heterodoxies, this view on their stances might come as a surprise and as an objectifying critique of their critique. However, our aim here is not to side with either the heterodoxies or the orthodoxies, but to treat both positions in the same analytic scheme, reflecting as well on the position(s) we take up as Scandinavian researchers.

Standards or tougher selection of candidates?

Creighton (2002) addresses the standards movement critically in his journal article with the catchy title *Standards for Education Administration Preparation Programmes: Okay, but Don't We Have the Cart Before the Horse?* The suggestion is that standards (the cart) are unnecessary or even veiling the fact that mediocre candidates (the horse) are entering the preparation programmes. What good are standards if the real problem is the candidates selected for educational administration?

More specifically, based on existing statistics as well as a review on selection criteria from 450 colleges and universities, Creighton finds candidates in educational administration programmes from 1996 to 1999 to have:

> attained GRE scores (Graduate Record Examination) ranking near the bottom when compared with 41 graduate fields. Compared with seven specific education majors, education administration ranked second from the bottom in verbal reasoning, third from the bottom in quantitative reasoning, and second from the bottom in analytical reasoning
> (Creighton, 2002, p. 529).

In other words, candidates in the educational administration programmes are not selected as rigorously and as carefully as Creighton suggests they should be, with the horse in front of the cart instead of the other way around. Candidates in educational programmes even score lower than candidates in other education majors, such as elementary education and secondary education. This finding seems to contradict the review by Crow and Whiteman (2016) in the sense that is does provide (some discouraging) knowledge of the background of the candidates. Similar findings have been pointed out earlier by McIntyre (1966; cited in McCarthy & Forsyth, 2009, p. 89), who stated: 'The average student of educational administration is so far below the average student in most other fields, in mental ability and general academic performance, that the situation is little short of being a national scandal' (p. 17).

Creighton's suggestion to strengthen selection is stated rather unreflectingly. He discusses (p. 539) whether the problem is the selection of candidates or in fact the recruitment of them, but the full implication of the latter is not discussed. If the demand for school leaders exceeds or equals the number that can be recruited (attracted), being tougher on selection seems impossible. The situation is similar to what was described in Chapter 2 via Lortie (1969) in the case of teachers: due to society's 'chronic demand' for teaching, teachers can never evolve into a full profession. They do not control the selection and training of candidates, which is essential to a (or an emerging) profession. The same seems to apply to school leadership.

Nationalisation of educational programmes

In a historically comparative study, Brundrett and Fitzgerald (2007) have described the nationalisation of educational programmes in the UK and New Zealand. This nationalisation took off in the 1990s with the invention of the Teacher Training Academy and the National Standards for Headteachers in the UK and has since been intensified and strengthened. New

Zealand seems to follow the path laid out by the UK, resulting in more similarities than differences between the two countries.

Brundrett and Fitzgerald are generally critical of this development, although their criticism is expressed in a careful and covert way. They warn against 'uniformity' and 'orthodoxy' in the supply of school leader education and training. Moreover, they discuss trends towards compliance, conformity, and implementation of top-down models as leaving no room for the academy and scholars like themselves. They point towards some of the knowledge, competencies, and ideals this orthodoxy seems to squeeze out, including education as opposed to training, theory-praxis nexus as opposed to 'what principals need to know', collaboration as opposed to dominance, and reflective knowing and higher order cognitive abilities as opposed to standards and standardisation.

Even if we concur with Brundrett and Fitzgerald in many respects, this dichotomisation of positives and negatives may also indicate the stance and position they take in the game of school leadership. In order to play this game and be as successful as possible, opponents seem to be portrayed more crudely than they necessarily are, while sympathisers and followers are portrayed more positively than they need be. In other words, frontiers are sharply drawn to demean opponents and glorify allies. This seems to be the name of the game as well for heterodoxies.

Leaderisation and standardisation

Not so covert is the critique by Gunter (2016), who deploys the term 'leaderisation' to denounce neoliberally driven reforms which, in her view, accord too much significance to leaders and leadership at the expense of teachers. In so doing, they transform the very notion of school leadership. This critique and the position from which it emanates is similar to what was described in the previous chapter on the knowledge base (Gunter & Forrester, 2009).

More specifically, leaderisation is claimed to have 'forced a shift from professional agency to prepare and develop understandings of educational roles towards the structuring impact of training and licensing for reform delivery and audits' (Gunter, 2016, p. 28). This means leaderisation not only transforms the notion of school leadership (as understood by Gunter) but leads to a process of deprofessionalisation, as claimed also by English (2006). Rather than professional autonomy, agency, and discretion, which are normally seen as key features of professions and professionals (cf. Chapter 6), leaderisation stresses external means of control, such as licensing and audits.

In terms of education and preparation, Gunter writes an 'intellectual history' to describe the consequences of leaderisation on the traditions, purposes, domains, contexts, and networks in this sub-field (she uses the same framework here as was developed for the analysis of the general field, cf. Chapter 3). She finds leaderisation to permeate all aspects. As regards traditions, for example, she claims the field to be dominated by 'how-to-do-it "programmes" in texts, software, and training that focus on "hot topics" and provide the busy practitioner (not necessarily a qualified educational professional) with clear instructions and guidance on how to deliver externally determined reforms' (Gunter, 2016, p. 33). As another example, the purpose of school leader education or, rather, training is circumscribed by functional and situational perspectives aimed at not educating the professional practitioner but 'fixing' what needs to be done and removing what is deemed dysfunctional, for example, by inspection officers.

Many of the same shifts have been pointed out by other critical scholars in the field (e.g. Tomlinson et al., 2013; Simkins, 2012; Young & Brewer, 2008). In Australia, Eacott (2011) has stressed the damaging effects of standards. These lead not to an increase in quality, outcome, achievement, or the like but to standardisation. Instead of standards, Eacott argues:

> The doxa of school leadership needs to be more than challenged, it needs to be resisted. This requires a leadership habitus that is not just about having learnt the rules of the game, rules which have established the principal as the deliverer of the agenda of the state. . . . The time is now and I encourage others, whether they identify as scholars or practitioners, to not sit by as a passenger but to actively engage in the struggle for education. After all, our children deserve it.
> (Eacott, 2011, p. 59)

These are rather lofty but not necessarily wrong arguments for reclaiming education and school leadership. At the same time, they can be analysed as stances expressing and seeking to expand a specific position within the field.

The Danish and Scandinavian context

The Nordic education programmes for school leaders are quite similar in content and organisation, although differences can be discerned. In general, the programmes are focussed on leadership development. They are not preparatory, designed around internship and a prerequisite for leader appointment, as is the custom in the USA, the UK, and Canada (Kommunernes

Landsforening, 2017; Moos, 2013; Uljens et al., 2013). In the Nordic countries, recruitment and appointment typically happen within or among schools in a locally defined career path from middle management to headship. Formal education and development come next.

The programmes vary in length, structure, and level, but, as a rule of thumb, the duration is one to two years (part-time, while working as a school leader), between 30 and 60 ECTS, and at a master's level. In Denmark, school leader education for primary and lower secondary school is at the bachelor's level – but with a maximum of 60 ECTS.[3] In Sweden and Finland, school leader education is compulsory at all levels, whereas it is only compulsory in Denmark for primary and lower secondary school. In Norway, school leader education is not compulsory, but in many places (especially the bigger cities), it has gradually become the norm. Providers are normally universities or university colleges, but private companies have recently entered the market in Denmark through state-controlled systems of accreditation (Uddannelses- og Forskningsministeriet, 2020).

Instead of attempting a more elaborate description of the Nordic school leader educations, including research in the field,[4] we present instead some paradigmatic cases which can show some of the aims and span of content. The cases are deliberately chosen to show differences and tensions. This may yield a description where lines are drawn more strongly than is necessarily the case in everyday life.

BI: school leader education and training for primary and lower secondary school in Denmark

Normally, school leader education and training for primary and lower secondary school in Denmark is managed by two national programmes: Diploma in Leadership (DIL) and Public Education in Leadership (DOL). Municipalities and school leaders are free to choose which of these basic and overlapping programmes they will attend, with DIL being the latest and most autonomous or school-like and DOL the oldest and closest to practice and employer perspectives (Weinreich, 2014).

In two Danish cities (Aalborg and Copenhagen), however, school administration has decided to educate their school leaders at the BI Business School in Oslo, Norway. BI has developed a specific master's programme for school leaders. The programme is inspired by the American school effectiveness movement. Databased leadership, student learning and assessment, and a goal-oriented performance culture are among the subjects taught.[5] Hattie, Robinson, Helmke, and Nordahl constitute a large part of the literature. During the courses, the students work with databased leadership as an instrument for preparing school changes in their own schools.

Critics claim BI is not in line with the Danish school leader traditions, which have a broader focus on the leader's roles and tasks. BI education also does not take place at a university college, but at a business school, which is uncommon in a Danish context (at primary and lower secondary level). This implies a specific perspective on leadership which tends to be focussed on results and effectiveness (Pasgaard & Malkenes, 2017).

MIG: school leader education and training for upper secondary school in Denmark

Another case is our own master's programme for upper secondary school leaders in Denmark, the Master of Upper Secondary School Pedagogy (MIG). This programme is provided by the University of Southern Denmark in the Faculty of Arts.[6] The programme was established in 2000 and caters to both teachers and leaders. In practice, teachers and leaders are divided into specialised tracks supplemented by common and crossing themes. The aim was to develop a programme where education was rooted in the context, problems, and challenges characterising upper secondary school in Denmark – as a contrast to generic leader programmes found in other schools and universities.

Where the curriculum at BI could be described as narrow, homogeneous, and inspired by the school effectiveness movement, the curriculum at MIG is broader and more heterogeneous. The curriculum is inspired by classic ideas and approaches within the arts and within critical sociology. It could be compared to what Ottesen (2016) in Norway has described and argued for as a pedagogic knowledge base of school leadership.

The purpose of MIG is to educate – not train – the participants so they can reflect on present tendencies in leadership and educational policy and compare these to their local conditions. The idea is that the participants must be educated as unique leaders, not as reflections of the previously mentioned tendency towards leaderisation (Gunter, 2016). Furthermore, the aim is to educate leaders to perform professional discretion in cases of insecurity and indeterminacy (Bøje, 2017; Grimen & Molander, 2008).

Nordic school leadership in tension

The two cases represent very different views on school leader education and training. From a historical perspective, the BI leader education programme represents a new tendency in Danish school leader education. Expressed in the previously developed notions, it represents the orthodoxy of international school leadership. BI provides close instructional leadership, as described by Harris (2005), while MIG resembles interpretive leadership (see Chapter 3).

The two cases can be further elaborated by again referring to Møller (2016), as well as to Wiedemann (2021). Based on experiences from Norway, Møller (2016) has identified the way in which school leader education has been delivered the last 50 years. She focusses on theories and the knowledge base used. She concludes that an international discourse on steering and management has marginalised the former traditions of democracy, pedagogy, and humanism, which have also been prevalent in educational programmes in the UK and New Zealand (Brundrett & Fitzgerald, 2007). Empirical research, results, and internationally defined standards and criteria are the new knowledge base. Wiedemann (2021) has studied the textbooks used in Danish school leader education since the 1970s with the aim of identifying historically specific school leader ideals. With minor modifications, he identifies tendencies similar to those proposed by Møller (2016).

Thus, the 'good' school leader and the 'good' school leader education or training programme seem to be contested in the Nordic countries. The matter is under tension between previous ideals and more recent tendencies.

The importance of education to the professionalisation of school leadership

Where do these tendencies and struggles within the field of school leader education leave school leadership in terms of professionalisation? In this final section, we address this question and attempt some answers, recognising, of course, the preliminary and limited status of these. To give a more comprehensive answer, we need the other chapters in this book, which each cover a specific dimension of the professional project.

In the sociology of professions (cf. Chapter 2), the significance ascribed to education and training along with knowledge is usually high. This varies with the specific view on the professions (functional, power, organisational, or otherwise), with some giving higher priority to ethics and values. Nevertheless, education, training, and knowledge have overall been recognised as key features of the professions – features associated with modernity and separated from earlier forms of traditionalism, magic, and superstition. These rational and modernistic features can indeed be found in the knowledge base, as well as in the education and training programmes for school leaders. In particular, what we have referred to as orthodox or dominant positions exhibit these features. Looking to fill the gaps and improve the practice of school leadership, actors in this position typically rely on quantitative data and statistical analyses that show correlations between, for example, school leader education and student test scores.

This technical knowledge and its transformation to curriculum and standards does not seem to be connected to an explicit and elaborate attempt at professionalisation, however. We rarely find arguments or attempts to improve the education and training programmes of school leaders to do something other than improve, which typically implies an increase in student test scores. When 'improvement' is connected to 'professionalism', it is espoused by the heterodoxies in rather a negative way. Actors in this position reinterpret improvement and effectiveness as a loss of autonomy, agency, and discretion, thereby leading ultimately to a process of deprofessionalisation.

The standards movement could be interpreted as a willingness in the field to set aside differences and work together towards a unification of school leadership as a professional group. In Goode's terms, the standards movement could be a decisive step towards becoming a community within a community, including shared values, agreed-upon roles, common language, etc. (Goode, 1957, cf. Chapter 2). Certainly, this is the impression given when reading some of the works of the standards movement. As described, however, the heterodoxies reinterpret standards as standardisation, homogeneity as uniformity, coalition as political influence, etc. As such, the standards movement has yet to prove claims of unification and professionalisation.

Neither orthodoxies nor heterodoxies are particularly elaborate in their ideas of professions and professionalisation, let alone in their ties to education and professionalisation. Implicitly, they may be arguing from confusingly different everyday definitions. In other words, whether they agree on what to disagree on is uncertain. Viewing the matter from a Nordic perspective, the ideas, arguments, and writing by the heterodoxies come closest to what we normally perceive as professions and professionalisation – and deprofessionalisation: an ethics- and value-oriented conception which resembles that of the early Parsons (1951, 1954) and which interprets school leadership as a moral, democratic, and politically contingent endeavour rather than a neutral and technical delivery of narrowly defined results. Orthodoxies place greater emphasis on efficiency, but they also argue from a normative position, such as on behalf of underprivileged children who are assumed to be in need of standards-based forms of leadership. Both features – values and efficiency – are necessary to be or become a profession (cf. the development in Parsons' body of work), but different levels of importance can be attached to either one. This might explain some of the confusion and controversy between orthodoxies and heterodoxies.

A theme which cuts across orthodoxies and heterodoxies and which has equal impact on both is the (lack of) control of the selection, training, and entrance of candidates. In the sociology of professions, this control is assigned to the professions – the classic ones, that is (priests, doctors, and lawyers). Through this control, they can socialise new members into the rules, practices, and identities which account for the profession, and, most importantly, they can decide the supply, thereby remaining a distinguished group – a scarce resource. As suggested, it does not seem possible for school leaders to control the selection and entrance of candidates to this extent. Even if no chronic demand exists for school leaders comparable to that existing for teachers, politics will often define demand and supply. This might impair the ambitions of becoming a full-fledged profession.

Notes

1 Diana G. Pounder is former president of the influential American University Council for Educational Administration (UCEA).
2 (1) Mission, Vision, and Improvement, (2) Ethics and Professional Norms, (3) Equity, Inclusiveness, and Cultural Responsiveness, (4) Learning and Instruction, (5) Community and External Leadership, (6) Operations and Management, (7) Building Professional Capacity, (8) Internship.
3 www.ug.dk/uddannelser/diplomuddannelser/samfundsdiplomuddannelser/diplom-i-ledelse
4 Such accounts can be found in Moos (2013, 2016).
5 Utdanningsledelse: www.bi.no/studier-og-kurs/executive/skole-og-barnehageledelse/skoleledelse/?gclid=EAIaIQobChMIxOKY5c-E6gIVDomyCh1XcgcXEAAYAS AAEgKXrPD_BwE&gclsrc=aw.ds
6 www.sdu.dk/da/uddannelse/efter_videreuddannelse/master/master_gymnasiepae dagogik?gclid=EAIaIQobChMIxNC9x-Gk7AIVCiwYCh3-HAlXEAAYASAAE gICJvD_BwE

5 Ethics in school leadership

Professional ethics is another characteristic discussed in the sociology of professions and normally considered necessary for an occupation to qualify as a profession (cf. Chapter 2). Adhering to a professional code of ethics, as well as developing ethical awareness in praxis, is a prerequisite for qualifying as a profession. This applies to the individual members of a profession and to the broader community of practitioners. Furthermore, ethics can be expressed by the professional ethos of a professional group – for example, as ideals and values of care, charity, service, democracy, and Bildung. These ideals and values were more important than technical knowledge and training to the 'early' Parsons (1951). By contrast, for the 'elder' Parsons (1968), the balance shifted. More recently, Goodson (2000) has argued for a so-called principled professionalism in the case of teachers. This is a type of professionalism which reinstates values as the focal point to professions, particularly the 'people-processing' ones such as teaching.

How is ethics considered in school leadership? *Is* it considered as part of the attempt to professionalise, or is it instead ignored in comparison to, for example, pursuits of a solid knowledge base and elaborate education programmes? What could possibly be gained from a better understanding of ethics in school leadership? These are some of the questions we address in this chapter.[1]

The chapter illuminates the role of ethics in school leadership and discusses different attempts to establish a formal code of ethics. Furthermore, the chapter critically examines existing research on ethics and school leadership, including perspectives on effectivisation and ethical pressure; distributed leadership as either a relief or a reinforcement of ethical pressure; ethics and standards in postmodern times; and reflexive leadership. In terms of school leadership in Denmark, professional ethics is deeply connected to the fundamental objective of schooling, which is democratic formation (Bildung) as well as basic education. We investigate whether codes of ethics have been developed that reflect these aims. Furthermore, drawing on

DOI: 10.4324/9781003033257-5

examples from our own research (Hjort et al., 2018), we discuss ways in which school leaders can be simultaneously 'ethical but unethical' – that is, how they can adhere verbally to ethical codes of conduct but act differently in praxis. In conclusion, we point out ethical paradoxes and dilemmas for school leadership as an emerging profession.

Attempts to establish a code of ethics

Different attempts to establish a formal code of ethics can be discerned across the Nordic countries and in the international context. These vary from not so elaborate to highly elaborate, formal, and ceremonious. In the Danish context, no formalised code of ethics exists, but ethics is included in the professionalisation strategy mentioned earlier (Lederforeningen, 2008). Here, it receives substantial attention when values other than results and accountability must be specified.

A telling example can be found on page 2. Here, the Danish and internationally recognised professor of ethics and philosophy of religion, Knud E. Løgstrup, is quoted as saying:

> To create schooling is a meeting between people with different experiences, understandings, and expressions concerning a given matter. To create schooling is therefore something living and untameable which must not be confined by the inner nature of the school.
> (Lederforeningen, 2008, p. 2, our translation)

Translating Løgstrup for an international audience is difficult, but basically he is saying to create schooling, it must not be equated with the school in its institutionalised and rational form. People, education, and human meetings must not be reduced to a technical matter similar to machinery. Seeing this statement as one of the first pages in the Danish school leaders' professionalisation strategy is both interesting and telling. The quote is accompanied by an introductory clause that says:

> In a time where society sees it as most important to measure and quantify the results of children's schooling, it might be worth reflecting on K. E. Løgstrup's lecture given 23 years ago. One of the central points was that not all aspects of the school can be inscribed in simple plans, schemes, and grades.
> (Lederforeningen, 2008, p. 2, our translation)

This indicates the position of the Danish association of school leaders: results and accountability are important, but we must not forget other and broader purposes of the Danish comprehensive school. School leaders are responsible (not accountable) for these purposes and must work towards them in their everyday praxis. This is also evident from the fact that these purposes are (still) inscribed in the objects clause of the Danish basic school, where they are formulated as values of democracy, equality, freedom, and fantasy (Børne- og Ungeministeriet, 2020).

Moos (2016, 2017) recognises and frequently mentions these broader purposes as important to school leadership. He argues they have come under pressure from neoliberal agendas and school systems, as witnessed by a shift in the balance of the objects clause of the Danish basic school: today, qualification and training (section 1) rank above democracy, equality, freedom, and fantasy (sections 2 and 3).

In Norway, the largest association of school leaders, Utdanningsforbundet (2017), has developed a professionalisation strategy similar to the Danish strategy. It expresses many of the same ideas, values, and priorities, including professional ethics. This is understandable, given our common history and welfare state. To an even greater extent than the Danish association of school leaders, Utdanningsforbundet stresses its historical foundation and its continued relation to the teaching profession. In the Danish case, the professionalisation strategy is described as a 'supplement' to teachers' professionalisation strategy, whereas Utdannningsforbundet explains their paper as a chance to 'clarify' their work with respect to the work of teachers. At one point, they state:

> We belong to the teaching profession. Our community mandate [social contract] is to further day care institutions, pupils, and students' learning, development, and Bildung. We share the responsibility, and we share the task.
> (Utdanningsforbundet, 2017, p. 4, our translation)

This indicates a limited level of independence and a commitment to ethical values characteristic of teachers in the Nordic welfare states.

In the UK, the Association of School and College Leaders (ASCL) has produced a framework which describes seven principles of ethical leadership in education (Association of School and College Leaders, 2018). This paper comes close to a formalised code of ethics, whereas ethics in the Danish and Norwegian context occurs as a theme among others in a more general professionalisation strategy. The seven UK principles are (1) selflessness, (2) integrity, (3) objectivity, (4) accountability, (5) openness, (6) honesty, and (7) leadership (ASCL, 2018, p. 10). On the face of it, these principles seem similar to some of the values in Denmark and Norway, such as selflessness, which might express equality and democracy. Conversely, viewing the principles from a Nordic perspective, the inclusion of accountability and objectivity as ethical principles seems odd. As described above, accountability also occurs in the Danish professionalisation strategy, but not as an ethical value. Accountability and results are instead opposed to ethics, as focus areas necessary to the instrumental qualification and training of pupils.

Another difference between the British paper and the Danish and Norwegian papers is the role the papers are thought to play. In Denmark and Norway, 'purposes', 'values', and 'mandates' are described; in the ASCL paper, a 'framework', 'principles', 'standards', and 'clear examples' are described. For example, the committee representative, Jane Martin, offers the following comment in the foreword: 'As the Committee's representative on the Commission, it was encouraging to see the obvious passion to set a clear example to school and college leaders and offer guidance to help address the ethical challenges which are part of their role' (ASCL, 2018, p. 3). Our point is that ethics in a Danish and Nordic context is an action and a disposition, something to strive for, not a standard that can be implemented and used as a control stick. Furthermore, having a code of ethics is not guaranteed to ensure ethical conduct in practice. Ethics does not consist of the code itself, but rather of the leaders developing ethical awareness and praxis through continuous learning processes. A critical perspective will focus on whether the code becomes part of the leaders' professional ethos or an empty standard – in the worst case, a straitjacket.

Existing research on ethics and school leadership

Critical perspectives exist in the research on school leadership along more conformist perspectives, typically stressing the importance of ethics – and not much more than that. Some research describes ethics in leadership more generally. In the following, we review some of this research. We have selected and organised studies in themes which directly or indirectly address the question of professionalisation apart from ethics.

Effectivisation and ethical pressure

One central theme has been termed 'ethical pressure', which usually is related to political governance and effectivisation strategies. The ethical dimension of school leadership involves several phenomena that have a dynamic character and a number of symbolic components (Conger, 1998). School leaders are at the forefront and bear the responsibility for acting ethically sound. This implies 'establishing and maintaining emotionally safe and ethical workplaces' (Tenuto et al., 2016, p. 11).

However, strategies of effectivisation challenge the nature of ethics, and standardisation and test systems counteract professional integrity and autonomy in decision-making among school leaders, as well as among teachers. The cost-conscious, data-driven approach to societal makeover leaves school leaders and their staff vulnerable to ethical pressure. This happens when tensions arise between deeply held values and the external demands of effectivisation and management.

Some of the ethical challenges school leaders encounter in their work arise due to the tension that exists between political management, a formalised code of ethics, their personal leadership, and a complex and challenging field of work:

> Protagonists present management concepts as universalised knowledge that fulfils desirable goals by following the ideas and prescriptions proposed. But what happens when decontextualised knowledge developed in one context travels across contexts and is recontextualised?
> (Hagedorn-Rasmussen & Klethagen, 2019, p. 92)

From an ethical perspective, the top-down initiated efficiency strategies are a challenge to creating value-based and ethically sound leadership based on professional virtues, care, and involvement. These conditions create a complex kind of ethical pressure, forcing school leaders and teachers to account for disparate and contradictory considerations. The processes produce an increased demand for organisational learning for both teachers and leaders. Raae (2020) finds a number of studies to have emerged which investigate how leaders handle pressure. Still, the subjective conduct of leaders and facilitation of organisational learning are underrepresented in existing research. As Fuller (2012) argues:

> Practice is shaped by the dominant managerialist educational leadership discourse that emphasises accountability and surveillance in a neoliberal marketised and technicist school system. It is only by looking beyond that and by enacting the people-oriented values they promote in schools that headteachers model them for others, thus demonstrating their care.
> (Fuller, 2012, p. 686)

Can unacceptable ethical pressure erupt in the processes of change and implementation of school reforms? This may be the case. A way out of this is to have the courage and competence to stand on values which challenge New Public Management. Weinberg and Banks (2019) argue that, in times of an 'unethical climate', it is imperative that professionals practice what they define as everyday ethical resistance, opposing ethical and organisational pressures. This is also stated by Fuller (2012, p. 672): 'Some headteachers simultaneously work within a managerialist system and beyond it to promote people-oriented values ... headteachers are willing to resist aspects of managerialism to ensure that diversity is not only catered for but is also celebrated'. Thus, school leaders need to be engaged in identifying the ethical nature of their work, determining underlying values, assessing facts (scientific evidence), identifying relevant virtues, and using moral imagination (Bezzina, 2012, p. 263). Alternatively stated, ethical leadership consists not only of the code of ethics, but in the ability to translate values and ethical positions into practice.

Distributed leadership – a relief or reinforcement of ethical pressure?

Another theme concerns the much-demanded idea of distributed leadership (described more extensively in Chapter 3) and its relation to ethics. Distributed leadership has historically developed from an analytical approach to a more normative approach, which is a method or tool considered desirable in schools. Following this more normative approach, does the concept lead to more ethical leadership, or does it, on the contrary, reinforce ethical pressure?

With the rise of distributed leadership, the ethical demands and challenges for school leadership have followed. On the one hand, the ability to create positive learning environments that involve all actors in learning communities is an aspect of authentic leadership (Avolio & Gardner, 2005; Duignan, 2014). On the other hand, implementing distributed leadership is a long-term project that requires organisational and cultural change towards security and trust-based work environments. These processes are accompanied by ethical learning processes and organisational learning through which basic values for schooling can be transformed through new forms of coaching and networking (Alvesson et al., 2017).

Harris (2008) and Spillane (2005, 2006) suggest that an increasing but, at the same time, continuously challenged attentiveness to managerial values exists as part of the transition to distributed leadership. The decentralised management structure; the personal values of the leaders; and the political, organisational, and institutional values are often in conflict. School leaders thus experience ethical pressure due to political, municipal, and state-led reform processes through which new trends and standards for management influence prospective recommendations for qualification and optimisation of school management worldwide, as '[m]anagement concepts travel across contexts' (Hagedorn-Rasmussen & Klethagen, 2019, p. 92).

Several ethical considerations and potential unethical consequences arise in connection to the transition from solo leadership to distributed leadership (Crawford, 2012). The rise of distributed leadership originates from a top-down management tool despite its cooperative design and democratic intensions (Hjort et al., 2018, p. 106). The new managerial structures have not been implemented from the position of a free choice among teachers and leaders. Thus, distributed leadership is not necessarily a guarantee of better ethical leadership. On the contrary, it can lead to a higher degree of ethical pressure because managerial responsibility shifts and disappears into a more diffuse form of organisation.

Ethics and standards in postmodern times

Some researchers stress the postmodern condition in which welfare societies and schools are continually and rapidly changing (Duignan, 2014). This condition renders probable an increased focus on the context and support for leadership (Avolio, 2010). Educational reforms are a loosely coupled and complex system which, contrary to rationalist and market-driven logics, reinforces a necessary ethical focus on human relations to a greater degree than centrally decided standards and conformity (Derrington & Larsen, 2012; Goldspink, 2007). As argued by Duignan:

> I believe a general evolutionary trend is discernible, starting with a focus on self (know thyself, to thine own self be true); to considering and defining self in relationships; to accepting that there is a moral force behind notions of self-fulfilment; to recognising that authentic leaders operate in a real post-modern (perhaps post-postmodern) world of pressures, paradoxes and ethical challenges – especially, in a world of standards and accountability for performance outcomes.
> (Duignan, 2014, p. 166)

Granted that a postmodern or post-postmodern condition exists and defines our way of life, the current attempts to define standards and streamline school leadership seem paradoxical. How is this possible if conditions change continuously and rapidly, if context is key, and teachers are co-leaders? Perhaps the current attempts to standardise school leadership should be understood exactly in light of these conditions: rather than relaxing, the noose is tightened – or attempted to be tightened – until the next context and a plethora of demands arise. As argued in the following chapter, professional discretion, including ethical consideration, may prove a better means of dealing with the postmodern condition.

Reflexive leadership

Cultural change, organisational change, and new forms of work and management are fundamentally relationally borne (Avolio & Gardner, 2005).

Work pressure and efficiency pressure (Raae, 2020), and thus ethical pressure (Ribers, 2020), may increase on leaders at different levels, but a greater degree of self-management, creativity, and co-determination may at the same time be developed through reflexive leadership. Thus, reflexive leadership is a fourth and additional theme to be reviewed.

Avolio (2010) argues prospective development in leadership involves processing and reflecting upon one's self, behaviour, ways of leadership, and interactions with staff and stakeholders rather than following a particular style or behaviour. Ribers et al. (2021) point out four elements in teachers' and leaders' professional development and learning of ethical awareness: (1) the existential-phenomenological dimension, (2) the life-historical dimension, (3) the dimension of interrelational competence, and (4) the social dimension of learning. Through an interchanging dynamic between subjective experiences and dialogical learning, ethical perception is accentuated in the perception of leadership practice:

> Ethical agents need to be encouraged to develop their dialogical competences and capacities for moral discourse, beginning with becoming wide-awake to the ethical issues and challenges that permeate their day-to-day work lives and for which they must assume significant subjective and objective responsibility.
> (Cherkowski et al., 2015, p. 15)

One approach to educational development through democratic procedures is action research and related research methods that involve a developmental element which can help to understand and define the visionary value level and sustain development of leaders' ethical awareness (Gavino & Portugal, 2013). Action research in organisations and in education has the potential to develop leadership as well as teachers. Through action research, there is an opportunity to bridge the gap between the code of ethics and the realities in practice.

The fundamental problem between the high demands of ethics and leaders' opportunities to comply with these can be elucidated and discussed, and new solutions can be developed collectively. In line with this, Alexandrou and Swaffield (2012, 2014) suggest that educational leaders should advance and develop both personally and professionally. Action research holds the potential to integrate the personal, the professional, and the political dimensions (Noffke, 1997).

The question is how critical ethical reflection and dialogue are developed and enforced. How does moral perception become part of the awareness that ensures leaders do not uncritically become agents of discursive and political trends? Leadership is largely a human practice based on relationships that demand value understanding, self-reflection, self-knowledge, self-criticism, and professional integrity (Crawford, 2012). Ethical dilemmas will inevitably arise due to differences between personal values and professional and organisational values, but one solution is to promote ethical reflection in decision-making processes (Kimber & Campbell, 2014). Research can encounter difficulties in getting to the heart of the problem for school leaders, but with lengthy action research, new insights can arise in addition to new opportunities for action.

Ethical but unethical – examples from research

An important theme in Danish research on school leadership is the tension that exists between the visions and ideals of ethical leadership and the grey zones which characterise praxis. In the following, we present some examples from our own research (Hjort et al., 2018) to show how this tension may be narrated, reflected on, and handled. Among other things, the examples illustrate how school leaders might state ethical intentions but act in ways which seem unethical, thus presenting themselves as simultaneously ethical and unethical. The examples are derived from a specific part of our research project – namely, that which focussed on leader networks and coaching. Here, ethics became a major issue.

When school leaders follow new management trends, such as the development of personal leadership, this can compromise several of the humane, collegial, and organisational considerations discussed above. Our research (Hjort et al., 2018) shows examples of how school leaders in public forums expose vulnerable and confidential information about employees, as well as about other leaders, as they construct a narrative about their personal leadership. Concurrently, the research shows that, for some school leaders, whether they acted ethically or not has not been a significant consideration.

One of the core elements of ethics is whether trust is honoured or broken at an interpersonal level. A school leader says the following about trust in an organisation:

> We work with trust because it requires enormous trust in the organisation for us to succeed . . . we as management expect trust from our employees, but our employees must also have trust from us. I think there is trust at stake because otherwise it could not be done.
>
> (our translation)

According to this school leader, trust is a two-way communicative act and is the foundation of ethical leadership. It is an unarticulated and invisible ethical demand which implies: 'We take care of the life which trust has placed in our hands' (Løgstrup, 1997/1956, p. 18).

Another school leader states that the development of networking and coaching loses its ethical relevance if trust, intimacy, and community are not present:

> It is not worth anything if the leader network is a place where you go to assert yourself. One can say that trust – some may be more indifferent than others with this – but it is important to be able to enter the network and believe that here I can say exactly what I want. Here I receive help. Or here we have the same problems and others want to contribute. That is essential.
>
> (our translation)

What the quote emphasises is the importance of the collectively rooted and trust-based, reflexive leadership. Anchored in this trust-based relationship are the ethical demand and ethical responsibility (Løgstrup, 1997/1956). The leader goes on to elaborate that: 'There must be a lot of trust in the organisation before you dare to expose yourself and enter a new learning space'. This indicates that trust in interpersonal relationships and in organisations are a prerequisite of ethical leadership. As again explained by Løgstrup:

> Trust is not of our own making; it is given. Our life is so constituted that it cannot be lived except as one person lays him or herself open to another person and puts him or herself into that person's hands either by showing or claiming trust. By our very attitude to another we help to shape that person's world.
>
> (Løgstrup, 1997/1956, p. 18)

Ethics in school leadership can be challenged by managerial strategies and typologies. This becomes problematic when professional ethics is not explicitly elucidated or thematised with the dichotomies, problems, and dilemmas that arise between the influence of external political governance and the internal human and relational aspects of praxis. Our research shows school leaders experience great help and benefit from coaching and management networks, but the fact that networks also involve a difficult handling of personal information presents a new challenge which can lead to unethical conduct.

Through interviews with school leaders, we studied their views on the networks and forms of coaching they had been involved in. We did the same via a survey that also investigated the leaders' assessment of whether competition between individuals and schools, career plans, and school policy alliances can lead to breaches in confidentiality. The research showed a discrepancy between the results from the interviews and the results from the survey. In the survey, 71% disagreed there should be a risk of dissemination of sensitive personal or institutional information. In the interviews, the participants recognised the issue and called for ethical rules of the game – that is, guidelines for networking and coaching activities (Hjort et al., 2018, pp. 104–105).

Furthermore, when asked in the survey what the strength of the networks had been, 85% agreed it was the fact they could speak freely and exchange experiences with leaders in similar situations. When later asked whether the leadership networks worked better when not assembling colleagues or representatives from competing schools, 48% agreed. This again points to a discrepancy, with some answers (37%) indicating the networks had in fact not been so open and free as previously stated. When asked in the survey whether the networks had lacked clear guidelines for network practice, 86% of the leaders stated they were content with the existing guidelines. This also contradicts what was said in the interviews (Hjort et al., 2018, pp. 104–105).

The overall conclusion of these findings was that an ethical awareness among the involved school leaders had not fully emerged. This does not mean they did not lead from a perspective of humanism, values, and visions; however, verbally and cognitively, the following important themes could not be traced: ethical pressure, moral distress, and duty of confidentiality. Thus, the research shows a need for further attention to ethical awareness and praxis (Hjort et al., 2018, p. 118).

Confronting ethical dilemmas collectively – other examples from research

Findings from an action research project (Ribers, 2020) can shed light on ways in which some of the above described dilemmas can be handled – collectively. When school leaders experience and confront ethical and unethical practices, either their own or those of others, it highlights the importance of engaging in self-reflective dialogues regarding values and visions for the organisation as a whole. If this competency is manifested and collaborative values are created, this can be regarded as an expression of a collective ethical consciousness and conscience (Pruzan, 2001). In other words: 'Ethical responsibility is not only an individual concern but equally collective and organisational' (Ribers, 2020, p. 10). When professional ethics is viewed and expected to be solely the responsibility of the individual school leader, then ethical pressure and moral distress may emerge. This points to a need for strengthening an understanding of ethics as a field of contradictions and dilemmas, as well as a requirement for extended development through action research that enhances ethical reflection in educational programmes for school leadership.

Being an innovative school leader involves moral imagination (Bezzina, 2012) and visionary engagement in future practice – even though ideal practice is contested. Hence, ethical dichotomies can constitute a potential for development. When school leaders confront ethical dilemmas, the opportunity arises for shared ethical reflections that can facilitate key ethical learning processes, as well as managerial and social change processes. In this way, school leadership becomes a question of how to create an ethical organisation culture (Alvesson et al., 2017).

When high ethical ideals can hardly be complied with under the existing control of schools, this can be experienced as ethical pressure by the individual school leader. Thus, ethical pressure – understood as the inability to live up to personal and professional standards – can lead to moral distress and ultimately to stress, burnout, or compassion fatigue. Professional ethics is not solely a question of normative behaviour within specific institutional frameworks. Schools are becoming increasingly diverse, and cultural differences bring ethical norms into conflict with each other. This development adds another level of complexity in terms of professional integrity and responsibility (Hightower & Klinker, 2012). To act with professional integrity, continuous reflections – self-reflection and collective reflections – on the relationship between oneself and others are necessary.

A code of ethics and unethical praxis – paradoxes and dilemmas for the professionalisation of school leadership

In conclusion, ethics in school leadership consists of a number of factors: the codes of ethics at international and national levels, the code of ethics and the set of values that apply to a specific organisation, school leaders' personal values and moral perspectives, and the development of ethical perception and discernment through reflexive praxis. This also implies a need to develop professional virtues, such as courage, empathy, righteousness, and trustworthiness.

The role of ethics in school leadership is imperative, yet the design of formal codes of professional ethics differs vastly in various countries in terms of how far principles and standards have been developed and how strongly these have been implemented in actual praxis or embraced by school leaders. In other words, ethics in education and leadership is also a matter of ethical and unethical organisations. The school culture governs the working environment, and the most central part of school reform is cultural change.

Hence, a paradox is constituted by the top-down initiated implementation of distributed leadership. It necessitates attention to the kind of value-based management the schools exercise and the extent to which it is top-down or bottom-up.

When we look at existing research on ethics and school leadership, the most prevalent trait is the dichotomy between ethics and governance. The increasing focus on effectivisation places ethical pressure on school leaders. Similarly, new trends in managerialism, including the makeover of distributed leadership, can, in some cases, reinforce ethical pressure. In line with these findings, we see that school leadership in Denmark is characterised by a clash between professional ethics, which is intertwined with one of the key purposes of schooling – namely, democratic Bildung – and attempts to streamline and render more effective school leadership, which is intertwined with today's most dominant purpose of schooling – namely, qualification and training. It seems imperative to develop codes of ethics reflecting and discussing both these aims.

How can ethical codes of conduct be integrated into school reforms and become part of the awareness of school leaders? Ultimately, ethical values and principles can form the collective ethos of an emerging profession and be a means to perform everyday ethical resistance – a way for school leaders to counteract neoliberal school regimes. The important role of ethical aspirations in postmodern times, based on codes of ethics, is closely interlinked with reflexive leadership. Leadership networks can be considered ethical communities that anchor leadership in sound ethical practice. As new forms of leadership develop in interaction with external contexts, the type of training that takes place outside one's organisation will also change. The professional ethical values and principles may or may not be opposed to demands of accountability and marketisation. Quite often, leaders find themselves in a grey zone between being ethical and unethical, as illustrated by our examples from research. This causes paradoxes and dilemmas that the attempt to professionalise school leadership must take into consideration.

Note

1 Some of the points and examples in this chapter draw on results from the Danish research project 'The Qualification of School Leadership (2016–2018)' conducted in collaboration among Katrin Hjort, Peter Henrik Raae, Anja Hvidtfeldt Stanek, Jakob Ditlev Bøje, and Bjørn Ribers (see Hjort et al., 2018).

6 Working conditions and work life

A recent account in a Danish newspaper from a now retired school inspector, Flemming Mortensen, describes how the position, which is now entitled 'school leader' (not school inspector), has changed over the past decades: 'There will never be one like me again', he concludes (Risbøl, 2020). The former inspector states a remarkably increased central steering currently exists, as well as less dialogue between decision makers and the school staff. Furthermore, a test regime and more goals are affecting teachers' work. 'Come and talk with us and gain knowledge through conversation rather than searching for it through standardised questions, taken from an Anglo-Saxon school system that does not look like ours at all', Mortensen states. This development, as described by Mortensen, is in many ways paradoxical. On the one hand, school leadership is emphasised as a crucial factor for school development and signals that school leaders must have greater opportunities for leading and setting directions in strategic, pedagogic, and financial matters. On the other hand, the experience of many school leaders is reduced autonomy due to an increased level of political and administrative intervention (Bjørnholt et al., 2019).

The story by the now retired school inspector illustrates how the requirements and expectations of school leadership may have changed, affected, and restricted possibilities to conduct professional judgement. This complex or even contradictory development is an international phenomenon, although with variations among different countries (Neeleman, 2019). As a school leader, one must take a wide range of different stakeholders into account, including teachers, parents, administration, and communities that often try to influence the decision-making process. In this often tense and contradictory field, school leaders must try to practice professional judgement.

The aim of this chapter is to illuminate relations between the insights from previous chapters concerning perceptions on professions and professionalisation, the foundations of a knowledge base for school leadership,

DOI: 10.4324/9781003033257-6

and endeavours for education and preparation of school leaders and the situation where school leaders meet or continue in their practical day-to-day circumstances. What are their conditions for making decisions? How is school leadership controlled by internal or external constraints like economy and politics, and does this control leave room for autonomy as is usually claimed in regard to professional work? Their practice and local contexts are among other causes affecting professional development. Do patterns in the development of conditions and their practice support a tendency towards professionalisation?

In the following, we describe the development of various aspects of assigned autonomy appearing concurrently with various forms of inspection. Subsequently, we discuss concepts of school leaders' decision-making and exercise of professional judgement. Then, we employ cases which illustrate recent empirical tendencies and perceptions among Danish school leaders concerning a reform of basic school. Finally, we summarise and provide a conclusion regarding the consequences for the professionalisation of school leadership.

On the concept of autonomy

The concept of autonomy is closely connected to the perception of professions and professionals, as discussed in Chapter 2. In the sociology of professions, the general assumption is that a professional's performance depends on a high degree of autonomy. This is important for making decisions and performing actions on behalf of clients. The literature covering the theme of this chapter does not generally draw on the sociology of professions. In some cases, an everyday understanding seems to characterise the concept of autonomy, assuming it simply to be something 'present', 'necessary', or 'good'. Our approach consists of following the literature some way along, while maintaining a position in the sociology of professions.

One of the main dimensions of a school leader's working conditions is established in the relationship between schools and the legislative authorities. In that respect, most countries have experienced remarkable changes over the last decades. The overall tendency has been a movement from state regulation towards more independent schools in a more competitive environment. Parallel to the increased independency, and as described in the introductory paragraph, audit procedures have increased in return. Among the main reasons for this development is the 'downsizing' of the welfare states and the upturn of New Public Management in various designs and expressions. Christ and Dobbins (2016) widen this explanation by adding concurrently happening societal trends – what they refer to as *post-materialism*, where 'classical materialist values are being replaced by non-utilitarian values such as self-realisation, quality of life and authentic political participation' (p. 365). These trends tend to support a decentralisation process, and Christ and Dobbins conclude that this approach has been underrated compared with the more common explanation with a central steering chain starting with the OECD. Christ and Dobbins also assume and tentatively find that one can distinguish between two overlapping governance models in the decentralisation process: the participation model and the competition model. The competition model is directed to promoting quality and enabling schools to strategically position themselves, thereby giving more school choice. The participation model aims to 'democratise' school policymaking by incorporating local stakeholders. Christ and Dobbins assume that centrum-right systems prefer the first model while centrum-left systems lean towards the second. Countries do not follow the same path, and neither the situation before nor the situation after are similar.

A problem occurs due to the circumstance that an adequate definition is missing. Furthermore, the meaning and discourses have changed over time (Heffernan, 2018). This means that tracing tendencies towards professionalisation of school leadership may be difficult. However, we will illustrate definitions, and we will attempt to clarify in what areas one may find a degree of autonomy. Autonomy, according to the dictionary, is defined as 'self-governing', which, in turn, means 'functioning without the control of others' (Levacic, 2002, p. 187). The unresolved element in this definition is what *control* means and who is to decide the level of external control. Or is a perception of control sufficient? Neeleman (2019) takes this definition inside the area of schools and mentions that 'school autonomy is defined as a school's right of self-government – encompassing the freedom to make independent decisions – on the responsibilities that have been decentralised to schools' (p. 34).

Other variations may also exist between these general definitions and the actual practice in specific school systems and specific schools. Little is known about how schools in different countries actually use their decision-making authority. Some enlarge the definition and have interpreted autonomy in a twofold manner as both the freedom and capacity to act, or they have focussed on capacity. This points to a general consideration that might be taken into account. Attempts to enhance school autonomy do not necessarily lead to autonomy in practice. This might suggest that the general definition is supplemented by the combination of freedom and the capacity to act – that is, how autonomy is enacted in schools (Neeleman, 2019).

What are the areas for autonomy?

One crucial step would seem to be to identify what areas in schools autonomy is assigned to or perceived in relation to. Variations might exist for starting a new educational programme, for training programmes for teachers, or for installing a new smartboard in the classroom. To take another example: do leaders have possibilities for making strategic choices concerning the size and composition of student cohorts?

OECD conducts an autonomy index. They have given a definition of the areas that these decisions are concerned with for comparable studies. They are (1) organisation of teaching (e.g. student admissions, lesson times, choice of textbooks, constitution of classes, teaching methods, and daily assessment of students); (2) personnel management (e.g. hiring and firing of teaching and nonteaching staff, salary tables, and influence on careers); (3) planning and structures (e.g. the opening or closing of schools, design of study programmes, choice of subjects taught in a specific school, and creation of qualification exams for a certificate or diploma); and (4) resources (e.g. allocation and use of resources for teaching staff, nonteaching staff, capital, and operating expenses (Cruz Martins et al., 2019). Cruz Martins and colleagues take these figures and analyse several aspects of school autonomy, and one of their main conclusions was a scattered pattern. They found a tendency towards more autonomy in the Nordic part of Europe and a more centralised tendency in the south, but the pattern was not the same for all affected areas.

Another contribution to a division of areas was made by Christ and Dobbins (2016), who, in their analysis of the development in Western Europe autonomy, include dimensions from Rürup (2007; cited in Christ & Dobbins, 2016). These dimensions contain elements including (1) organisation of instruction (i.e. design of the learning environment, such as learning groups, instruction time, and scheduling); (2) personnel management (i.e. selection, deployment and management of personnel, human resource development, the selection of pupils, school management and committee structures, and personnel and pedagogical oversight); (3) financial matters, such as distribution of resources, financial obligations (e.g. contracts), and accountability measures; and (4) resource and facility management, such as procurement, administration, and maintenance of school buildings and facilities, classrooms, and teaching and learning resources.

Neeleman (2019) attempts to investigate school practice and derive changes during a period of increased autonomy: what interventions have happened and are they considered? Intervention is, by far, not an unambiguous phenomenon. In a Dutch context considered to have a high level of autonomy, also according to the OECD index, Neeleman conducted surveys and interviews with school leaders and gathered answers from almost 200 upper secondary school leaders to deal with the considered weaknesses of general classifications. From this, she investigated in what areas schools took initiative and completed interventions in their own schools. She ended with three broad domains of 'education', 'organisation', and 'staff', and a total of 16 subdomains. The strength of a study like this may be its provision of a more detailed picture of a school's possibilities for making decisions. A weakness is the reduced possibility of comparisons with other systems. Neeleman also states the more autonomous system in the Netherlands compared with other countries with tighter regulations as another potential limitation.

However, commentators (e.g. You & Morris, 2016) notice attempts at defining autonomy, for example, by the OECD, are too vague and conceptually ambiguous for application to a single country, not to mention a single school. Current indicators used to capture school autonomy are insufficient and give rise to flawed conclusions. Furthermore, as Heffernan (2018) mentions, the policy documents that discuss principal autonomy are broadly descriptive in nature and provide little detail on how autonomy might be enacted in practice. A common feature of many of these accounts is that the personal and institutional dimension is important for how the possibilities are utilised. Similar regulations may have various other outcomes.

In many contributions, autonomy for schools is an implicit point of departure. Nevertheless, in some, two aspects of autonomy can be observed – namely, autonomy for the school and autonomy for the school leader. A widely used report is that of Adamowski et al. (2007) concerning the autonomy gap and focussing on the leader autonomy. One of the main issues in this report is the possibility of rewarding good teachers and firing ineffective teachers as one of the most important tasks for school leaders and a significant indicator of autonomy and decision power. This may be a more general assumption in school leadership. A success criterion – or a main precondition – seems to be a separation from and distance to the teachers (cf. Chapter 7).

The differences between countries may be caused by variations in steering chains. These could be boards, superintendents, county councils, etc. This means that school autonomy and decentralisation add new relations to school governance, to the extent that they open up new channels of influence to a broader array of local, regional, and internal school stakeholders (Christ & Dobbins, 2016) – actors who previously were excluded from influence.

Accountability in return

The generally increased level of autonomy is followed by an increased focus on accountability. The accountability systems may also vary considerably between countries. Hammersley-Fletcher et al. (2020) have compared the process in one high autonomy, high accountability, and high stakes context, England, with one low autonomy, low accountability context, Turkey.

Besides these general differences, one of the findings by Cruz Martins et al. (2019) was the similarity of the unsystematic variances in the assigned and perceived autonomy – the variances in auditing systems were just as unsystematically varied.

The changed competition may, on a macro level, have generated a negative outcome by increasing the levels of social segregation and stratification within the education system – with already privileged schools thriving in this environment while less-privileged schools being left to flounder and fail. One outcome, as referred in Keddie (2015), is that the shift in accountabilities was 'self-defeating' because it forced many schools to only concentrate on things that are measured, such as achievement in the formal auditions.

School autonomy is often connected to outcomes for students. In some cases, a relation might be noted between the achievement of results and an assigned autonomy: better performance, more autonomy. In Heffernan's analysis of school leader autonomy in Australia, a principal supervisor described the process of working with principals who were deemed to be underperforming, noting that 'principals who have been unable to bring around improvement will naturally attract more support – more attention, more capability development, and more intervention' (Heffernan, 2018, p. 385). This might be interpreted as an instructive or educative function connected to 'governing at a distance', so when school leaders are sufficiently mature, they might be given more freedom. This might also be amplified by a personal dimension, as principals who have longevity at their schools are said to have more bargaining power (Adamowski et al., 2007).

We are not able to derive from the literature an operational definition and a subsequent description of the situation in the single country or school system. In general, central regulations are decreased, but in various manners concerning what areas will be assigned local decisions. We have also seen various systems of accountability, usually for the purpose of comparison and ranking, but the reasons vary. The areas for comparing autonomy to a wide extent seem to be linked to the implementation of a given policy rather than affecting the same policy.

The development in the last few decades may be seen in light of two lines in New Public Management (Hood, 1991) - namely, a dimension inspired by the market leading to competition and a contractual dimension leading to accountability. In both dimensions, the school leader is still portrayed with great emphasis as the main person responsible and the key to delivering expected results. The accountability dimension contributes to both contracts and market. Schools are confronted with contrasting discourses, which focus both on increased autonomy and new ways of recentralisation or neo-governmentality.

On the concept of professional judgement

The general, though varied, changes in governance structures in educational systems might be leading to changing and various conditions for school leaders to make decisions. This is important for the understanding of possible characteristics of professional development. What does professional judgement mean in a school leader context?

Central to a traditional approach to professionalism is the professional judgement or discretion. Grimen and Molander (2008) distinguish between two elements of discretion. On the one hand, discretion may be defined as a cognitive process of reasoning involving a mediation of knowledge on the basis of incomplete information in new situations. On the other hand, discretion can be regarded as the professional's negatively defined freedom to make decisions within a more defined scope, which, for example, enables a choice between a number of different standardised methods. This definition indicates that professional judgement concerns the ability to make independent choices based on experience and knowledge. Sometimes autonomy or the lack thereof limits possibilities for discretion.

This approach is closely related to the concept described by Dewey (2011) for intelligent judgement and nonrational decision theories. Dewey's concept stresses that habits are social norms of behaviour or the reason to act. Habits may change over time, leading to changes in the organism and subsequent changes in the environment. Furthermore, the concept of experience is important: 'When we experience something, we act upon it, we do something with it; then we suffer or undergo the consequences' (Dewey, 2011, p. 78). In other words, we do something to the environment just as the environment does something to us.

Experience enables us to see how things are connected. Experience leads to realisation. You can gain experience from trying things, using the trial-and-error method. This develops intelligent habits or intelligent judgement. The embeddedness of experience is also central to an institutional approach to decision theory, developed among others by March (1991). Decision makers (e.g. school leaders) do not have knowledge of all possible decision alternatives, the consequences of these, and their preferences for the future condition after the decision. Although decision processes are usually intentional, they rarely are goal rational. Rationality is limited, and the decision makers usually seek to attain the most appropriate decision guided by experience, institutional norms, expectations, and their values (cf. Chapter 5). To a large degree, one relies on tacit knowledge developed through practice and experience.

Some have tried to develop operational concepts for use in educational contexts. Hargreaves and Fullan (2012) have developed a concept of professional capital, which consists of human, social, and decision capital. Social capital is the most important and consists of trust and collaboration in the workplace. Human capital refers to individuals' knowledge and competencies, as well as empathy, among other things. Decision capital involves the ability to make professionally sound decisions in connection with daily tasks and in the face of complicated situations. Although the concepts are interrelated, decision capital is especially relevant here. A prerequisite for having a high decision-making capital is that one is in possession of knowledge capital and, in many cases, social capital.

We have now delineated the concept of professional judgement. In summary, it presupposes experience and professional knowledge, but also the ability to relate analytically to problems in the everyday environment. Professional judgement requires a certain degree of autonomy and is affected by institutional and social norms and values. These might be more or less regulating and applied in different areas.

Consequences of leaders manoeuvring in changed frames

The literature tends to point out that school leaders have gained more autonomy and decision power, but this comes with new forms of accountability and restrictions. Whether the room for manoeuvring is large or little, good or bad, is impossible to say. Christ and Dobbins (2016) refer to some of the main positions in educational research. Proponents point to purportedly more efficient decision-making and resource utilisation, diversification of education, local innovations, and a stronger democratic character of education. These factors are, in turn, expected to improve educational outputs and quality. Conversely, opponents worry about aspects such as duplication of administrative structures, barriers for diversification due to accountability, an unwarranted influence of interest groups, and the aggravation of social inequalities when competition changes from a means to an end.

The actual development may be interpreted in different ways by school leaders and commentators. The outcome may roughly be understood as either positive or negative. The answer to the question of whether school leaders have gained more or less power to make decisions has, in some cases, turned out to be positive. A quote from a school leader in a free academic school in England, and according to the inspection authorities (Ofsted) a well-performing school, tells the following:

> I think autonomy and the idea of giving schools and their Heads power over their own school in theory is a good thing. I really do. I think that that can't be a bad thing, if it's done properly and morally, and ethically. It's like Spiderman isn't it – with great power comes great

responsibility. You could have schools that are manipulating things for their own benefit.

(Keddie, 2014, p. 503)

This possibility leads also to the opposite possibility and opens a door to a new space for professional development: how to act in a competitive setting. Further accounts in Keddie's paper reveal that some academies do appear to be mobilising their new freedoms in improper ways. The aforementioned school leader states they are 'manipulating things for their own benefit' rather than for the benefit of students to look more appealing in relation to external measures of school success. Some evidence suggests that some academies are manipulating their student admissions criteria so that they can 'cherry-pick' more able students in order to improve their results. In general, well-performing schools in an Ofted sense attain more autonomy. They have proved their worth. Low-performing schools are not capable of handling this responsibility alone.

Other positions will claim other perspectives. One of these is Adamowski et al. (2007), who emphasise an imbalance between the responsibility assigned from central authorities and the actual possibilities school leaders have for making decisions on various problems. The authors describe school leaders' lack of possibilities as Spiderman reversed: with great responsibility comes not more power.

In the endeavour of creating strong leaders and strong leadership, a difference might emerge between educational systems with relatively unambiguous success criteria like rankings and league tables and other systems with more various purposes. The restrictions in the possibilities to conduct leadership may be perceived differently according to the education system in which a school leader operates. The ability to make judgements and the power to make decisions (i.e. to possess autonomy) depends on the areas where it seems possible or expected to actually make decisions. These areas may typically be related to hiring and firing teachers and other staff, the economic and financial aspects of the school, student recruitment, and defining the curricula. Most of all, the school leader is perceived as an implementor of policy reforms, and, in that perspective and steering chain, may be perceived as a middle leader.

Empirical tendencies

How do school leaders perceive their autonomy, and how do they enact this feature? Exactly what school leaders do in their line of work is difficult to determine. What actions do they carry out, and what decisions do they make? Is there a mismatch between what they ought to do and what they actually are doing? This lack of knowledge might be an obstacle for the possibilities to derive patterns and changes in school leaders' work during periods of changed political views on education. It might also be an obstacle for the endeavours aimed at creating more effective school leaders according to a standardised knowledge base (cf. Chapter 3) and more standardised leadership education (cf. Chapter 4). This might be seen as a change from a situation we do not know to a new situation we do not know either.

Several investigations have been conducted on the work done by leaders and managers starting in the 1950s (Gronn, 2003). Many approaches have been used, and a common feature of the studies is a row of methodological and conceptual challenges. The methods vary from more or less systematic observations, end-of-day questionaries, and interviews. Many of the problems are well known (e.g. what does one [not] see by observations, what is going on in the minds of leaders, what are they doing when not observed, how do they report their jobs, etc.). Despite the difficulties of knowing how leaders make decisions, the task still seems important. In the next section, we employ a current and relevant case from Denmark describing a reform of basic school and the resulting higher expectations of school leaders, changed relations between leaders and teachers, and changed governance structures. The empirical material is not from our own research, but from an evaluation conducted in parallel to the implementation of the reform (Kjer & Jensen, 2018; Kjer & Rosdahl, 2016).

The case of a school reform in Denmark

Thus, we will illustrate changes and dilemmas through a case describing a major reform of the basic school in Denmark in 2014. This reform was implemented simultaneously to the passing of a law which regulates teachers' working conditions. This law 409 was passed due to a conflict that hindered a new general agreement. Central to the reform of basic school was a focus on leadership, with an emphasis on governing by numbers, goals, and results. Likewise, the intention was to strengthen school leaders' autonomy (e.g. to plan the teachers' schedule and decide the direction of the school both pedagogically and strategically). Characteristics of New Public Management were evident in the reform, such as the orientation towards numbers and results and the focus on 'strong leadership' (Hood, 1991). Furthermore, the reform was coupled to the international trend where the school leader must be an instructional leader (Harris, 2005; Robinson, 2011).

Several evaluations and reports have been conducted showing the impact of the reform (Kjer & Jensen, 2018; Kjer & Rosdahl, 2016; Kjer et al.,

2015). Though the experiences so far are ambiguous, we describe some tendencies which are important to the attempt of professionalising school leadership. These tendencies point to various issues which are not mutually exclusive. The methods used are mainly surveys and interviews with teachers and leaders in the Danish basic school.

Generally, Danish school leaders report an increased workload following an increased number of tasks imposed by the reform. Traditionally, the Danish school system has been rather decentralised in the sense that the state has delegated authority to municipalities. Many school leaders report variations in relation to the municipalities, as some offer ostensibly more autonomy than others. Various areas seem to exist for autonomy, not least an economy specified as new financial concerns and regulation of teachers' workload. This leads to the interpretation that new conditions require new leaders, as predicted in the initial quotes from the former school inspector. The picture of being a CEO in a company has been used.

School leaders must also, in many ways, interact with and behave as actors in the municipality. This is illustrated by the following quote: 'I think I am drawn into significantly more municipal initiatives which I have very little influence on. It is school activities, but also municipal activities along with more personal requirements than before' (Kjer & Jensen, 2018, p. 15, our translation). Many stress this as necessary and feel comfortable with it. Some claim they are a kind of official or middle leader in the steering chain, and they identify as much with the municipality as with their school. The changed conditions seem to challenge the tasks and roles for school leaders, as one leader stresses: 'One gets tied up on some results in a completely different way than before. I think it becomes a kind of new generation of leaders to grab with' (Kjer & Rosdahl, 2016, p. 94, our translation).

At the same time, they have to stay closer to teaching, and they are subjected to an increased level of regulation through goals and measurable targets. This may, in many instances, lead to limitations in the declared autonomy. If the figures do not seem satisfactory, external authorities keep a closer eye on the school, and this decreases the freedom to act (Bjørnholt et al., 2018; Bjørnholt et al., 2019; Kjer & Jensen, 2018). This seems in line with the abovementioned conditions for the assigned autonomy, which depends on the ability to deliver results: 'If the subordinate level performs well, it gets or maintains a significant level of autonomy. If the performance deteriorates, the superior level interferes, i.e. the autonomy is reduced' (Kjer & Rosdahl, 2016, p. 93, our translation). A school leader illustrates this. Asked if the room for manoeuvring has become larger, the leader replies: 'Much bigger, really – if I live up to the requirements' (Kjer & Jensen, 2018, p. 13, our translation). A consequence of this development may be that the single school leader perceives less autonomy in setting the agenda and direction of the school.

In this way, autonomy may be understood as a floating signifier – in this case, a function of how well a school performs according to the governing authorities. We saw a corresponding interpretation in the English Ofsted environment.

Leaders reported difficulties in finding time to work with teachers due to the myriad of other tasks and responsibilities forming their workloads. Another school leader explains:

> I have been surprised at how much all the demands from outside take up in the daily work. . . . We have to go through what I have planned even though it is linked to what is also the requirements. But then something comes up all the time, or not all the time but often. Something comes up that takes time.
>
> (Kjer & Jensen, 2018, p. 16, our translation)

Another intention in the reform, and an essential part of the mentioned law 409, was to increase authority among school leaders to decide on teachers' working conditions. This issue was one of the main reasons for the missing general agreement, and it led to several conflicts around the country. Eventually, many municipalities entered into local agreements between school leaders and teachers and handled the original intentions of the reform more pragmatically. In the latest national working time agreement (2020), the school leaders' authority to decide on teachers' working hours has largely been lost. Instead, there will now be dialogue and agreement between the parties. This follows new governmental initiatives which highlight local freedom and school autonomy. One can argue that the earlier mentioned competition model has been challenged and partly replaced by the participation model.

The case of the Danish basic school reform from 2014 illustrates that reforms seeking to give school management more autonomy for independent development and change in schools can encounter difficult conditions and have outcomes other than those expected. The case also illustrates how the changed and ambiguous expectations of school leaders might affect these leaders' perceptions of their tasks and ultimately themselves. It seems obvious – or at least likely – that school leaders are becoming other kinds of leaders compared with the school *inspector* referred to at the beginning of the chapter. Lastly, the case illustrates that, besides struggling with political interference and control, school leaders also have to deal with teachers seeking to maintain their professional autonomy and privilege. Thus, teachers and their traditionally strong unions (at least in the Nordic countries) may represent another impairment in the attempt to professionalise school leadership.

Conclusion

The main purpose of this chapter was to analyse and discuss how current working conditions affect school leaders' work life and, more indirectly, what bearing this might have on the attempt to professionalise school leadership. The international trend represents a movement towards less central regulation and more independent schools in more competitive environments. This movement is closely followed by inspection and accountability systems that provide comparisons and rankings. Furthermore, a greater focus is placed on leadership and leaders' responsibilities in terms of school performance.

Some important conclusions can be made based on these tendencies. The treatment of autonomy is somewhat different in the literature on school leadership compared with the approach in the sociology of professions. Although often implicit, autonomy is not perceived as a feature of a profession or as a feature of the individual practitioner. Rather, it is located in the organisation (i.e. in the school). Consequently, school leaders do not simply regard each other as members of the same profession, but as competitors representing threats to and possibilities for a school market. The organisational definition of professions, as described in Chapters 1 and 2, may be better at capturing this understanding of autonomy, but this does not turn school leadership into a full-fledged profession, at least not according to the sociological definition used throughout this book. According to this definition, the current working conditions do not make room for the occupation to become a 'community within a community' (Goode, 1957). There is not sufficient autonomy. Politics, governance, and market logic define too much.

However, this is characteristic of other emerging (or semi-) professions as well (e.g. teaching, nursing, and social work), and the current lack of autonomy should not prevent school leadership from seeking a professional status. Autonomy, like trust, is a privilege to be earned, not something that can be claimed or simply taken – and it may take a while to earn, as illustrated by the cases of teaching, nursing, and social work.

The increased attention to and expectations of school leadership has led to school leaders working on many tasks and areas at the same time. The main tendency is that school leaders must make decisions on matters which were previously not a part of their job (e.g. finance). At the same time, many school leaders experience restrictions on matters that used to be their sole responsibility (e.g. teaching). Due to a staggering workload, they have difficulties in finding time to listen to and work with teachers. This tendency is reported internationally. Furthermore, interaction with teachers is affected by external authorities, as results are followed and monitored. This makes possible new conditions for decision-making.

7 Formation of a professional identity

Professionalism and professionalisation involve not only objective structures and forces, such as the knowledge base, education, and working conditions. Being or becoming a profession is also about the people performing this work. Who are they, what drives them, and how do they perceive themselves and their work? What professional identities do they pursue, and are they, in Goode's (1957, cf. Chapter 2) terms, bound by a sense of shared identity?

Compared with other subjects covered in this book, school leaders' identity formation is not the most researched theme. However, some research has been published showing, for example, the dilemmas and problems school leaders may face in the intersection between welfare systems and New Public Management. Other research focusses more narrowly on the 'new' leader identities crafted in private/corporate schools. A third group of studies is preoccupied with conceptualising the idea of a professional identity.

We review some of this research in the following, but this is not the main aim of Chapter 7. Rather, we devote most of the chapter to three school leaders' stories about themselves and their schools.[1] We analyse these stories as narratives showing sensemaking (Weick, 1995) and identity formation in the making, so to speak. The narratives also provide insight into some of the constituents used to construct narratives and professional identities. These are prior experiences as teacher, recruitment (preparation), education, training, and situated practice. The narratives show how these constituents are differently emphasised and interlaced in the three school leaders' narratives.

First, we review some of the existing research on school leader identity. We then analyse the three school leaders' narratives. We follow this with a summary, and we discuss how identity may constitute a lens for assessment of the overall attempt to professionalise school leadership.

DOI: 10.4324/9781003033257-7

Existing research on school leader identity

As mentioned, one group of studies has focussed on the tensions, dilemmas, and options available to school leaders in the intersection between welfare systems and New Public Management. Employing Bourdieu's concept of hysteresis, Courtney (2016) has described matches and mismatches – or disjunctions – between school leaders' habitus and current field conditions in England. Hysteresis is described as a state which occurs if a particular group's habitus is de-privileged and 'left chronologically stranded, its dispositions out of sync with the new rules' (Courtney, 2016, p. 3). What Courtney more specifically has in mind is the group of 'welfarist' school leaders who are unable, and, to some extent, unwilling to tune into the tones of New Public Management, including new ideas of corporate schools, connections to trust partners, hierarchical governance of teachers, and independence from local authorities. As an example, Courtney uses a crafted narrative from a school leader named Less. His story expresses pain and struggle and shows how ideals of democracy, equality, altruism, and care for 'difficult' children are gradually becoming hard to maintain, considering changed field conditions. These include Ofsted inspections and school closings: Less has twice experienced a school closing due to failure to meet standards, a problem related to the students' socioeconomically 'difficult' background at Less' schools. As opposed to Less, Courtney also crafts Paul's narrative. He is described as a 'corporate' school leader moving up the career ladder from an education in a public school with 'bog-standard' to becoming a school leader in free schools, a boarding school, and eventually headship in a school 'without history' – that is, a brand-new school opened by a coalition of trust partners without the usual ties to local authorities. His story is one of victory, self-confidence, and zeal – to the extent that he feels he needs to 'shake up the system' and counter habitus like the one maintained by Less.

Writing from a US context, Scribner and Crow (2012), based on a case study with a high school leader (Robert) in a reform setting, identify the various identities which must be developed and negotiated to achieve reform. This study is less preoccupied with power, struggle, and loss of meaning and identity and is more focussed on the possibilities a flexible identity may yield. Thus, working from a social constructionist perspective, acknowledging that ' identity is dynamic, multiple, contextual, embedded with degrees of ambiguity and/or certainty, and socially negotiated' (p. 247), Scribner and Crow develop five professional identities, each with a further series of constituencies or roles. These five identities are developed in relation to some of the contexts/audiences a school leader must stay close to and work with: (1) teachers, (2) students, (3) parents, (4) larger school/district, and

(5) community partners. Especially the first audience – teachers – is important to the studied school leader, Robert. His roles here include father, teacher at heart, and sergeant. These roles overlap and reinforce each other in a way where the educational background as teacher is generally emphasised:

> There are a lot of people that are administrators that couldn't teach their way out of a wet paper bag and that is a problem for me. I know lots of them. I know some of them that are on my campus. They have terrible relationships with teachers because teachers know they weren't good. They don't offer anything constructive for teachers from an experience standpoint. I know. I have been there. I know where they are coming from. Here is what I did. Here is what I have seen before. They don't offer any of that. They just offer punishment for what they consider is wrong.
>
> (Scribner & Crow, 2012, pp. 256–257)

In a way, this account comes closer to explaining what research into effective school leadership (e.g. Darling-Hammond & Rothman, 2011; Leithwood et al., 2004; Robinson, 2011) has stressed for a number of years – namely, the importance of an educational background as teacher. Through his experience as teacher – his teacher at heart – Robert can gain legitimacy vis-à-vis his teachers, something which is more difficult without that experience and something which Robert frequently encounters among 'administrators' at his campus.

Taking a Belgian context, Kelchtermans et al. (2011) argue stronger for principals' need to break with their former identity as teacher to assume a detached leader identity. This view is put forward in light of a high stakes context where 'tough decisions' are often necessary and where a strong and loyal relationship to teachers may impair such decision-making. Following this, Kelchtermans et al. attach importance to principals' emotional life, describing the strong feelings of loneliness, accusation, loss of identity, audience, and belonging that a principal, in their view, must learn to embrace. Practising distributed leadership and participating in leader networks and training programmes may soothe these feelings (cf. Chapter 5) and introduce the principal to a new audience whose connection can allow a 'stronger' and more demarcated leader identity to be built. In our following examples, we will return to this matter and discuss the professionalisation of school leadership as another audience or venture for the construction of detached/attached school leader identities.

Lumby and English (2009) focus on preparation programmes and the leader identities to which these programmes – explicitly and implicitly, knowingly and unknowingly – are connected. They, too, employ a social constructionist perspective, and they set out to deconstruct mainstream models of educational leadership preparation focussed 'on the acquisition of technical craft skills related to management and administration and socialisation into a generally uncontested set of values and norms' (Lumby & English, 2009, p. 96). These mainstream models, furthermore, rest on 'a largely Western, functionalist and unitary notion of the self . . . supported by metaphysical beliefs, as opposed to purely empirical determinations' (Lumby & English, 2009, p. 95). In other words, these programmes are popular and mainstream not because they are effective in the usual and explicated sense of the term, but because they work in subtle, mythical, and semireligious ways, 'baptising' students and narrating and leading them into the technical identities they eventually come to believe in. This underexposed process is one of the 'dark secrets' of educational leadership, according to Lumby and English. To attain more self-aware leadership, they encourage researchers, as well as practicians, to explore these secrets, including the role of norms and values. Describing and attempting to perform leadership as something like a technical drill is futile at the same time as it risks 'miniaturising' practice.

In Denmark, Moos et al. (2011) have conducted a study on the recruitment of school leaders, including a survey in which they ask about school leaders' background, motivation for becoming a school leader, relations to teachers and middle management, and importance of various internal and external tasks. They find Danish school leaders to generally have given up their teacher identity to assume a new identity as school leader. However, this finding is based on self-reporting, and the survey method does generally not permit evaluation of complexity, ambiguity, and hesitation to the same extent as an interview method, particularly narrative interviews. Most of the above referred studies are based on interviews, and this might explain their more nuanced findings. While Moos et al. find that Danish school leaders have become clear leaders, they still describe them as what Courtney (2016) refers to as 'welfarist' leaders; that is, they are leaders bound by the school's values and purposes in terms of skills and knowledge, as well as democracy, equity, and Bildung (cf. Chapter 5). The 'corporate' school leader is less prevalent in the study by Moos et al., and this is understandable with the Danish context and welfare state taken into consideration. Similar findings have been made in another Danish study (Klausen et al., 2011) on the public and decentralised leader (across the municipal system, in schools, day-care institutions, and elder nursing homes) and in a Swedish study (Nihlfors & Johansson, 2013) on the headmaster's role in the public governance chain.

Another and smaller group of studies seems to have moved beyond the depiction of complexity, struggle, and hesitation in the intersection between

Formation of a professional identity 83

welfare systems and New Public Management to instead focus on the new leader identities developed in private/corporate schools (Courtney & Gunter, 2015; Eacott, 2011; Rayner, 2018). Many resemblances are noted here to Courtney's 'corporate' school leader (Courtney, 2016) and to other descriptions in the above literature, but this group of studies appears to be plainer in its identification of corporate/private schools as dominating the UK, US, and Australian contexts. Consequently, they identify corporate school leaders as the new norm.

Speaking from a UK context and also based on interview data, Courtney and Gunter (2015) have described school leaders' vision work. This 'discipline' appears to be widespread, sometimes also referred to as strategising, and it implies the narration of strong and omnipotent leader identities ready to rule over teachers. Courtney and Gunter report cases where teachers happen to disagree with their school leader's organisational vision, or where they are disliked for some reason. Referring to these teachers, the studied school leaders frequently employ the metaphor of a bus – of getting on and off the bus. One school leader is quoted as saying:

> This is how it's gonna be. You're either on the bus or you're off the bus. And if you're on the bus, then we'll do everything we can to help and support you. But if you're not, then you're off the bus. And that's either through redundancy, through a restructure, through a change in roles, through a capability, through, 'do you know, what? This isn't the job for me, I'm applying elsewhere.
> (Courtney & Gunter, 2015, p. 411)

We are gradually becoming used to similar expectations and leader identities in a Danish context. Nevertheless, the above statement appears rather extreme. Respect for teachers and for democratic deliberation, including the right to criticise and disagree with your superior, is still the norm in the Danish and Nordic context.

A previously mentioned in Chapter 4, the study by Eacott (2011), reporting from an Australian context, also contains perspectives on educational leader identities. Here, leaders are described not so much as corporate and strong bosses, but as loyal deliverers of state-initiated reforms. 'Manager' and 'system representative' are other labels frequently used by Eacott, e.g. in the following way:

> The leadership of schools doxa present in the managerialist project structures the principalship with a delivery disposition. This disposition requires a surrendering of the public intellectualism inherent in school leadership as the principal becomes little more than the local

face of the systemic agenda. The embodiment of the school leadership doxa serves a reproductive purpose for the system as aspirants are habituated into the deliverer role.

(Eacott, 2011, p. 52)

Eacott's finding of this more governed school leader identity may be related to the fact that policy, rather than interview or survey data, is the empirical basis of his study. Policies and texts often represent expectations of someone and something rather than actual practice (Ball, 1994). Thus, Eacott also associates the 'loyal deliverers' with Taylorist and neo-Taylorist programmes (e.g. Total Quality Management and the professional standards agenda) telling them what to do, but not actually doing things in practice. Still, Eacott's study raises an important question as to what the relation is between the market side (the boss) and the state side (the loyal deliverer) personnel in New Public Management. In some countries and instances, the market side may be more strongly emphasised than the state side – in others, vice versa. In all cases, the two are connected as one strong programme influencing school leadership, as well as the school in general (Hansen & Bøje, 2017).

A third group of studies focusses on conceptually developing the idea of a professional identity (Cottrell & James, 2016; Crow et al., 2017; Gronn, 1999). This type of conceptual work can also be found in other and more empirical studies, some of which we have referred above (e.g. Courtney, 2016; Scribner and Crow, 2012; Lumby and English, 2009). The subject of a professional identity has also been discussed in the profession literature (e.g. Eriksen & Jørgensen, 2005; Heggen, 2008; Muel-Dreyfus, 2004). In this context, we concentrate on a study by Crow et al. (2017) that presents a theoretical frame for research on school principals' identities.

This study is based on the theories of Wenger and Bourdieu, accompanied by more empirical studies on the emotional dimension of identity. The article contains four sections, each dealing with a part of the theoretical framework summarised at the end. These sections are (1) the nature of identity: individually or socially constructed, (2) the emotional dimension; (3) understanding identity through constructing narratives; and (4) embedment in power relations, ideology, and culture. Roughly, the first section is informed by Wenger, the second by empirical studies, including Kelchtermans et al. (2011), the third by their own research, and the fourth by Bourdieu. At the end, the four sections are pulled together in a frame, stating:

(1) The narrative dimension: School leadership identity as temporally and socially constructed in the process of shaping a learning trajectory . . .

involves identity as a reflexive project and identity construction as a 'tool' for legitimation

(2) The epistemic dimension: The construction of school leadership identity as a cognitive activity, a kind of reasoning that results in judgements about what to do under circumstances of indeterminacy . . .

(3) The emotional dimension: School principals' identities for 'wearing and showing'; it involves identity as a dialogical struggle, the enactment of a ritualised role, managing and regulating emotions, and becoming skilled at 'impression management'

(4) The historical and cultural dimension: School leadership identity as a discursive practice reflects historically and culturally accepted patterns of behaviour. Normative discursive practices act as identity work, working their way into the professional lives of school principals . . .

(5) The political dimension reflects power structures within a national and local context: leadership identities are discursively positioned within the administrative field within education; it implies understanding the reciprocal interplay as the principalship is shaped by, and shaping of, the contemporary conditions where it takes place in time and space.

(Crow et al., 2017, p. 273)

In the following examples derived from our own research (Bøje & Frederiksen, 2019), we emphasise the first dimension – school leader narratives. Based on the leaders' narratives about themselves and their schools, we also discuss the historical, cultural, and political conditions in which these narratives have become possible and meaningful. Through our examples, we attempt to show the span between what might be called the first among equals and the generic school leader, including the experiences, types of schooling, and situated practices which have rendered possible each leader.

Becoming a school leader – three narratives

Our three examples of school leader narratives are informed by the so-called actantial model developed by the Russian formalist V. Propp (1984) and, later, the structural linguist A. Greimas (1973). This model (see Figure 7.1) is based on the idea that when we tell stories, we often compose these in terms of fairy tales. Furthermore, fairy tales typically revolve around six dimensions or actants connected in a certain manner: The young man (the subject) arrives at a kingdom from where the princess (the object) has been kidnapped by a goblin (the opponent). The king (the sender) promises the man who has the power and courage to free his daughter that he will get the princess and half of the kingdom as a reward. The young man sets out to

86 Formation of a professional identity

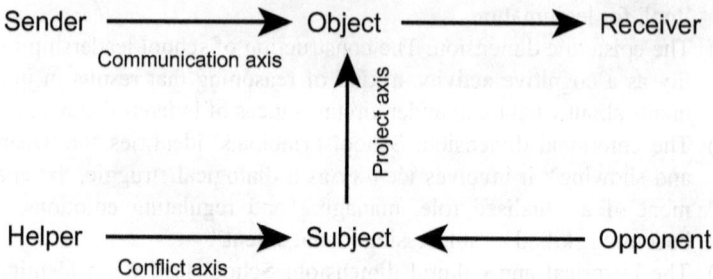

Figure 7.1 The actantial model

find the princess and on his journey meets a fairy (the helper), who grants him three wishes after having sent him on three trials. The young man finds the goblin and, using his three new powers, succeeds in killing him and freeing the princess. The story ends with a happy wedding and the young man becoming a prince (the receiver).

Our decision to use this model as a base for our analyses is founded on the fact that the three school leaders on their own accord told stories about themselves and their schools resembling legends and fairy tales. Preparing the interviews, we expected these to be conducted in a semi-structured way following a series of themes and questions worked out in advance. However, commencing the interviews was something like pushing a button, whereupon the leaders would talk and talk and talk about themselves and their schools, generally placing themselves in a starring role – hence, the idea to analyse the interviews through the actantial model.

The actantial model obtains for the structure of the narratives. To analyse the content, we look for what Riessman (2017) and Czarniawska (1998) refer to as the plot: the episodes and actions which bind together the actants and the overall structure of the narrative. To begin with, we present a short section on the biography and workplace of each school leader.

The first among equals – who eventually becomes a strong leader

Biography and workplace

Our first school leader, Kristian, is an experienced leader in his sixties who, at the time of the interview, was about to retire. Kristian was originally a teacher and maintained a position as such for about 15 years. He was then recruited to middle management. This happened in an indirect way, where

Formation of a professional identity 87

he 'grew' into management on the basis of union work and various representative positions. After six years in middle management, he became a school leader at his current school. Kristian has not obtained much formal leader education. In fact, he was a school leader for four years before he was admitted to a one-year course arranged by the local municipality. Since then, he has not obtained any further education.

When employed as a school leader, Kristian moved from one school (in which he was a teacher and middle manager) to another. This can be described as a move upwards, in that his previous school was situated in a socioeconomically and culturally more challenging neighbourhood than his current school. The pupils at his current school do somewhat better in the national tests than the pupils at his former school; the parents are better off financially and are more ethnically homogeneous; the housing surrounding his current school is composed primarily of villas, whereas the housing around his former school comprised social housing primarily. According to Kristian, more poor families have moved into his neighbourhood lately because cheap real estate loans have allowed them to do so.

Narrative

Kristian's interview conforms quite well to the standard definitions of a narrative. Compared to the interviews of the two other school leaders, Kristian's is quite long, and he is rarely interrupted by the interviewer. There is a beginning, a climax, and a happy ending; however, the ending is disrupted by some recent tendencies in the national education policy. In terms of genre, the narrative can be described as a drama in which Kristian is the hero who modernises the school and makes it more pedagogic and in tune with the pupils' needs, especially those of the socially disadvantaged children.

The narrative has two plots, one of which is overt and the other more implicit. The first and overt plot is about Kristian's modernisation of the school. He states:

> Well, one could say that the school was in a time warp when I took over. It wasn't like the fifties, but I started here in 1994, and at that time the school was definitely backwards in its view of teaching compared to the school I came from. In some ways, the view was effective, but it was that kind of teaching where one teacher has one class one hour at a time. There wasn't any cooperation or joint venture as regards the task of teaching.

He goes on to include characters (opponents and helpers) in the narrative (Greimas, 1973). The opponents are primarily teachers who are 'backwards' in their way of teaching. He explains they are backwards because they are 'spoiled' in the sense that the school's well-off pupils (and parents) have never forced the teachers to think and act pedagogically. Instead, the teachers have been able to maintain a school narrative in which they and the pupils are described as academically strong:

> I quickly discovered this school narrative which said that the school was an academically strong school. The norm among the teachers was that the pupils should always be academically challenged. And if a pupil was not very good, then more training and challenges were needed.

This academic school is opposed to the 'pedagogic' school which Kristian came from:

> I was used to working at the edge of things, you see. I came from XXXX, and there you had to be sharp. If you wanted to be successful, you had to know a lot about many things, not least pedagogy for guest workers, refugees, and persecuted people.

The following are the helpers in Kristian's narrative: (1) the poor pupils and their families who move into the area and put pressure on the teachers; (2) a research and development project with the Danish School of Education which was 'a bit of a surprise to the personnel. The analysis showed that the culture of the school was inappropriate. The school was divided in two instead of pulling together'; (3) the local school administration, which has supported Kristian both morally and financially; and (4) younger teachers and middle managers who are 'in tune' with Kristian's leadership: 'Everything I learnt about the staff led to the conclusion that I wanted to be 100% ready when we were recruiting new teachers and middle managers. They had to be in tune with the management of the school.' However, the most important actor in Kristian's narrative is himself. In the following excerpt, he describes how he became a more controlling leader than he had expected to be:

> And it turned out that there was a great need of leadership here. In this sense, I became a more controlling leader than I had expected to be. I had to control all the way down to the formation of teacher teams, who was with who, minutes during meetings, and development work, templates, what to do with data, how to summarise data, what future processes to set off, and so on. So, I guess you could say I got used to controlling a lot and perform the kind of leadership that everyone expects today. I think my development as a leader is exemplary of the

broader trends that have occurred within the management of the Danish school.

Another more implicit plot in the narrative concerns Denmark's current education policy. Kristian describes this policy as 'learning oriented', whereas he associates with a general education perspective (Bildung). However, he rarely criticises the policy openly. Instead, he makes comments such as the following:

> Well, this school is not doing particularly well in PISA. We have discussed this ... (laughs) ... because what happens when someone like them creates such ... such data? What can they show, and what can they not show? It has been uphill to get the nuances included.

He also states that 'if the data only measure the academic performance, and all attention is turned to that ... well, then you actually only live up to half of the school law. But I guess it's what's measurable that counts.' The laughter and many pauses, as well as the 'buts', 'wells', and generalisations (e.g. 'someone like them'), suggest that Kristian has difficulty in integrating this plot into his more pronounced hero narrative about the modernisation of the school. Thus, it can be considered a sidetrack or a so-called deviant life history that exists beneath a more conformist, dominant, and learned narrative (Goodson, 2008, p. 41).

To sum up, Kristian gradually narrates his identity into the kind of strong school leader 'everyone' expects today. Even so, his narrative and biography are marked by an identity as primus inter pares – the first among equals. Based on his long experience as a teacher and his interim period as union representative 'growing' him into management, he attempts to perform pedagogic leadership rooted in values and practices learnt in comprehensive school, including work with socially disadvantaged children. By virtue of these qualities, he attempts to lead and obtain legitimacy from his teachers, much like Robert and Less in the respective studies by Scribner and Crow (2012) and Courtney (2016). Thus, the two identities seem unsettled in Kristian's case, even if they appear in a sequence where the strong leader might have overlaid the first among equals.

In between

Biography and workplace

Our second school leader, Pia, is a relatively inexperienced leader who, at the time of the interview, was 46 years old. She was originally educated as a teacher, and she has worked as one for 22 years. Like Kristian, she made a step into management from a former position as a trade union representative. A short course called 'From Teacher to Leader', which was offered by the local municipality, played a significant role in this transition. She has not obtained any further leadership education. In 2009, she became a middle manager, and in 2014, she became a school leader. Thus, she had been a school leader for one and a half years at the time of the interview.

Pia is a school leader at the school where she also worked as a teacher. In other words, she has not made a move from one school to another in her journey to becoming a school leader. This is rather unusual in Denmark. The norm is to move from one school to another when you become a school leader. The school is situated in a diverse neighbourhood, and it recruits pupils from both the middle class and the working class. These pupils have ethnic majority and minority backgrounds. The housing surrounding the school is composed of villas as well as social housing. On average, the pupils perform slightly worse on the national tests compared to the pupils at Kristian's school.

Narrative

Pia's interview is more complicated than Kristian's. It is shorter, contains more breaks and questions posed by the interviewer, is more incoherent, and is even contradictory in places. Furthermore, it does not have a clear beginning, a climax, and an ending. Thus, the interview does not conform to the standard definitions of a narrative. However, it is structured along the lines of past, present, and future. In terms of genre, the main story can be described as a tale of the leader's suffering, struggle, and sacrifice to the school. This tale is supplemented by another story that is somewhat at odds with the first; it is closer to a fairy tale about a modern leader who reinvents the teachers, the school, and, one might add, herself. Generally, these two stories are not integrated, and one of them is not clearly dominant, as in Kristian's case.

The two stories are told through two plots. The first plot, which is related to the past and present, revolves around the running of a school that is situated in a mixed area. Pia states the following:

> The school is situated in an exciting neighbourhood, I think, which is characterised by great diversity. We have a big area for villas with families from the upper middle class: teachers, social workers, doctors, and those sorts of people. At the other side of the school, there is a big area for social housing, and until recently that area was on the government's list of ghettos. So, there is a certain mix of these

> two things. Also, it is a school for children with disabilities: learning disabilities, language disabilities, and so on. We usually say if you attend this school, you meet all parts of the Danish society. You get the full circle, so to speak. And, actually, we think it makes the pupils of this school very strong. They acquire a certain robustness. But it also demands a lot of the teachers who work here. They must be able to handle many things, including parents who have social or economic problems and parents who, on paper, should be great parents, but who are a little too involved in their children's lives.

According to this statement, the running of the school involves a number of challenges. On the one hand are poor and deprived families; on the other are wealthy families who make too many demands. Furthermore, the school is challenged by special classes for children with disabilities. To tell this tale about a challenged school, Pia employs certain metaphors (Spicer & Alvesson, 2011), which convey a sense of toughness and determination. In the above quotation, she talks about 'strong' and 'robust' pupils. Furthermore, she mentions teachers who must be able to 'handle many things'. When she describes herself as a leader, she employs similar metaphors: 'As leaders, we must be really, really clear about the direction of this school. We must communicate it clearly and through graphic images so that everyone knows the goal at the end of the day'. The idea seems to be that the school needs a *clear* and *strong* leader who is willing to make sacrifices and who perseveres despite challenges.

The helpers in this narrative are, first and foremost, Pia's middle managers and teachers. Thus, she talks about a united school, unlike Kristian, who tends to distinguish between good and bad teachers. Another helper in the narrative is what you might call 'the good middle-class parent' who joins the cause of the Danish comprehensive Folkeskole and makes an active attempt to help and integrate children who are less privileged than her own:

> We have some very educated and well-off families who help a lot: driving kids to and from football, offering an extra bicycle if we are going on a trip, and that sort of thing. Some kids around here don't have bikes, you know.

However, as indicated above, these well-educated and well-off families are, at the same time, opponents:

> A new challenge for the teachers is when a parent is all worked up on Monday morning and starts to complain about the arrangement of tables: that the tables are not placed in an orderly fashion or that the

arrangement does not suit the needs of his or her child. How do you reply to that kind of challenge? What do you do when someone like that crosses your professional boundaries? We have a challenge there that we try to handle.

Following this contradiction between the helpful and the demanding middle-class parent, a second plot and narrative can be discerned. It revolves around the future of the school. The middle-class parent also appears as a helper in this narrative, but in a new way. This time, he or she is not someone who joins the cause of the Danish Folkeskole but, rather, is someone who the Folkeskole must indulge and who, in return, helps the Folkeskole to achieve a brighter future. Pia explains this in the following way:

> For about ten years, the decision about open enrolment or free choice of school was made, and it almost tipped over the school. We were practically overrun by families from XXXX [a socioeconomically disadvantaged area], who wanted to get their children out of there. But then the previous school leader made some . . . and it wasn't a question of choosing some children over others. It was more a question of allowing local children to choose a local school. So, the leader and his managers made a short video that they sent home to all families, telling them what the school was like and so on. They also made brochures and information sessions so the parents would not make their choice of school based on what they heard on the streets. And it worked. Now, even families outside the area choose our school as their first priority. And socioeconomically, we think we have made a statement saying choose your local school instead of a private school.

Here, in a manner of speaking, Pia attempts to suture the ideology of the Danish Folkeskole (democracy, equality, and social integration) with the reality of the Danish Folkeskole – the past with the future, and the existing narrative with a new narrative. This happens by downplaying the conflict between these two entities – for example, the ambition to help socioeconomically disadvantaged children versus making a school for more educated and well-off families – and simultaneously constructing an argument about the right of local children to choose a local school.

Another and complementary theme in the second narrative concerns Pia as a leader and, more specifically, her leadership and vision of the school. She explains the following:

> Well, there used to be a different tradition at this place. My predecessor had another style of leadership. It was like, if you went into his office,

you would get a 'yes' or a 'no'. It was 'green' or 'red'. So, what we are doing now as a management team is to try and change that tradition – to ask, what do you think, what do you suggest, to get away from the directive leadership style and towards the co-managed organisation.

This nondirective style of leadership could be interpreted as incompatible with the clear leadership style previously warranted by Pia. She makes no attempt to integrate these two styles of leadership. Thus, the nondirective leader and the vision of the co-managed organisation seem to constitute another theme in the future-oriented narrative about a school overcoming challenges and preserving the core of the Danish comprehensive school.

Overall, Pia's narratives and attempts at sensemaking (Weick, 1995) may be characterised as incoherent and incomplete. In several ways, they reflect an undeveloped and unresolved position 'in between' – more specifically, a position in between the first among equals and what we will now describe as the generic leader.

The generic leader

Biography and workplace

Our third school leader, Louise, is also a relatively new leader. At the time of the interview, she was 39 years old. She was educated as a teacher, and she has worked as such for eight years. She was recruited to middle management at the school where she started as a teacher. Her school leader thought she had a talent for management. She has worked as a middle manager for five years. Meanwhile, she completed the one-year national education for public leaders (DIL, cf. Chapter 4) and commenced a master's in public governance. She has been a school leader for three years.

Like Kristian, she changed schools in connection to her employment as a school leader. This change can be described as horizontal, in that the two schools are quite socioeconomically and ethnically similar. Both are privileged schools located in relatively rich neighbourhoods, and both recruit pupils from educated families with ethnic majority background. Furthermore, the pupils do somewhat better in the national tests compared to the pupils at both Kristian's and Pia's schools.

Louise was recently appointed school leader at another school. Thus, she is, in fact, a school leader at two schools simultaneously. The new school is located at the outskirts of a large city and recruits pupils from mainly rural areas who come from less educated and poorer families than the pupils at Louise's first school. Furthermore, the pupils at Louise's new school do significantly poorer in the national tests compared to the pupils at her old school.

Narrative

The interview with Louise addressed her leadership at the new and rural school. Therefore, the narrative revolves around that. Interestingly, however, Louise connects her leadership at the new school with her leadership at the old school in many sentences. She does this in a fashion where the old school generally appears a model for the new school. Furthermore, the narrative about the new school is marked by the fact that Louise is merely an appointed leader. This means she has difficulty in taking a clear stand on many issues and, consequently, constructing a coherent narrative. She cannot very easily make 'causal relations' between episodes, characters, past, present, and future (Czarniawska, 1998, p. 3). However, Louise does tell a story along the lines of a past, present, and future. In terms of genre, Louise's story can be described as a fairy tale in which she is the philanthropic leader who saves (or attempts to save) a rural school from decline.

The story is told through a plot in which the transformation of bad numbers into good numbers is the starting point. Louise states the following:

> Well, it's a school that has struggled for some years to get the numbers up. Grade point average and so on. They have really struggled, and they have also had some success. But it's a school where many pupils are challenged and where their families are challenged. It's typically someone who settles here because the rent is cheap.

According to Louise, the problem of bad numbers also applies to sick notes, satisfaction measurement, economy, and crossover frequency to further education. In fact, the problem of bad numbers seems to be connected to a more general problem of culture – namely, rural culture:

> When I met the parents the first time, it was a bit of a strain. They sat with their arms crossed and looked quite sceptical. Of course, they were nervous that I would come and make their school into a XXXX school [a school like Louise's old school]. They had been promised by the municipality that it would not be so, that the two schools should remain separate. But that requires enough pupils, you know. And there aren't necessarily enough pupils in this area. The parents think it's nice with a small and cosy school where everyone knows each other and where it's their school more or less. But that's very costly, you know.

In the above quotation, it is possible to get a sense of the socioeconomic and cultural relationship that exists between Louise and the parents at her new school. It is a relationship in which the parents are looked down on and where the parents look upon Louise from an inferior and defensive position. While Louise often describes the parents and pupils based on what they lack, she also mentions what she would like to give them: 'This school is really worn out. Just look at it. Old furniture from the 1970s, ugly paint, outdated rooms, and so on. I would like to do something about that'.

More generally, Louise seems keen to supply the new school with the things that the old school has in abundance, even if she realises that the two schools are not the same and that she is merely an appointed leader. This includes her vision for the ideal organisation, which seems to have been realised at the old school:

> Here [at the old school], everyone knows me one hundred percent. The staff, the parents, and the pupils – they all know me one hundred percent. They know exactly what I want in every situation. Here [at the new school], they don't know me so well, so I must get used to communicating a lot. I also do that here [at the old school], but they know what I mean when I communicate. Here [at the new school], a lot of my communication is written – newsletters and that sort of thing. I rarely meet the staff in person and talk to them. So, it's difficult.

The above quotation is an example of how Louise often connects her old school with her new school, contrasting and comparing them. What seems to make the old school ideal, according to Louise, is the fact that the personnel know her so well. They even know what she might think or want in every situation. Thus, Louise emphasises the informal and personal aspect of her leadership, and she often uses metaphors that convey such a meaning.

Her opponents and helpers are easy to identify, which suggests they are dichotomously constructed. Opponents are referred to as 'rigid', 'concrete-like', 'cranky', or 'vulnerable'; they include teachers, parents, trade union representatives, and the teacher union in general. The latter is described in the following way:

> The trade union is always cranky. The local department is somewhat concrete-like. And the teachers don't use them. Not at all. The trade union has no general support. They are only for the cranky teachers. So, I think my idea is to turn the whole picture. Our greatest job as leaders is to make our staff great.

Helpers are described inversely in pure positive terms, as, for example, 'great', 'happy', 'funny', and 'co-managing':

> I try to work with this organisation [at the new school]. I try to make the middle managers great. I mean co-managing so they can make decisions themselves. It also applies to the rest of the staff. They must be able to make decisions when I'm not there. In general, I try to lead through leaders.

Compared to the two former leaders, Louise can be described a generic leader. This caption rests on several characteristics which seem to come together in Louise's case. First, she attempts to exert a kind of leadership applicable to both schools. This is, of course, a leadership informed by her experiences at the first and privileged school. However, this is never reflected or mentioned. Rather, these experiences are generalised to a point where they seem applicable to both cases. Second, Louise's vocabulary and narrative could be suggested to draw on words and discourses learned in a generic education programme – in Louise's case, a master's in public governance. As described earlier in relation to the study by Klausen et al. (2011), this programme spans across the municipal system – schools, daycare institutions, hospitals, nursing homes, etc. – and it may have supplied Louise with generic words and ideas such as 'co-management' and 'make middle managers great'. Third, in contrast to the two former school leaders, Louise does not talk much about teaching, pedagogy, purpose of schooling, or other subjects close to teachers. When referred to, it is often in an abstract language of 'raising numbers' or 'turning the school around'. This may be explained by her early recruitment for management, in addition to a rather short career as teacher. The teacher identity and, following this, the father/mother, teacher at heart, and sergeant in the study by Scribner and Crow (2012), does not seem to seem to be very developed in Louise's case. As such, it is possible to speak of a generic leader capable of leading several welfare institutions.

Identity as a lens to assess professionalisation of school leadership

These examples allow one to query about the consequences of professionalisation in terms of identity. As mentioned at the beginning of the chapter, professionalism and professionalisation involve more than objective structures and forces, such as knowledge base, education, and work conditions. Being or becoming a profession is also a question about the people doing the actual work. A tricky question in relation to the above leaders is who appears to be the professional school leader? On what grounds?

The analyses point towards the existence of an intergenerational dynamic involving an interplay between prior experience as teacher, recruitment, formal education, and situated practice. This dynamic is generally in favour of the generic leader. Leaders such as Kristian – the first among equals – may be on the way out of the Danish Folkeskole, as suggested also by the introductory example in Chapter 6. In fact, Kristian was ready to retire at the time of the interview. Thus, the generic leader may easily stand out as the professional school leader.

On the other hand, international studies stress the continuing complexity of identity formation among school leaders, and it seems likely the teacher-leader identity (the teacher at heart) will continue to be influential. Research into effective school leadership (e.g. Darling-Hammond & Rothman, 2011; Leithwood et al., 2004; Robinson, 2011) stresses the importance of this educational background.

Using identity as a lens to assess professionalisation of school leadership reveals that this project also entails normative and value-based questions. This was stressed in Chapter 5, but bringing in identity yields new perspectives. Thus, an inevitably normative question arises: what school leaders do we envision for the future? Leaders close to the lives of teachers and children, or leaders generalised from these actors, pulled towards each other and the external world in leader networks, strategy seminars, generic education programmes, market groups, etc.? Depending on the preferred answer, the specific nature of school leadership as a professionalisation project may be adjusted to that.

Note

1 We here rely on previous work (Bøje & Frederiksen, 2019) for which permission to reprint has been granted by Taylor & Francis Ltd, www.tandfonline.com

8 Professionalisation of school leadership?

In this book, we have taken a closer look at school leadership as a professionalisation project. We have departed from the sociological definition of professions, instead assuming school leadership to be an emerging profession rather than a full-fledged profession, and we have asked to what extent and in what ways this might be so. Viewing school leadership from other and competing definitions of professions (e.g. the everyday and organisational definitions, as described in chapters 1 and 2), school leadership may already be regarded and referred to as a profession. The professional associations of school leaders and many practitioners, as well as researchers, already do so. However, we wanted to scrutinise school leadership according to the norms, values, and criteria that have been used in comparisons of other occupations aspiring to professional status. We wanted to make school leadership responsible to this definition, so to speak.

In the following, we summarise the findings from the five main chapters constituting our attempt to analyse the professionalisation of school leadership: the knowledge base, education and training, ethics, working conditions, and formation of a professional identity. Based on this, we draw an overall conclusion. Finally, we discuss the implications of school leadership becoming a profession.

Knowledge base

In this book, we have pointed out the historic and current contributions which describe and, in themselves, constitute something like a knowledge base of school leadership. These include the theory movement; the standards movement; the managerial, transformational, instructional, and interpretive approaches to school leadership; the dominant, dominated, and emergent regimes of practice; and the Danish and Scandinavian contributions describing school leadership in a transition from universal welfarism to New Public Management and competition.

DOI: 10.4324/9781003033257-8

The theory movement, as well as its more recent variant, the standards movement, attempts to establish a science of school leadership. In most cases, this is done using statistics and correlations showing combinations between student performance (grades and test results) and different types of leadership, schooling, resources, etc. However, this attempt to establish a science has been, and still is, contested by many actors and by the fact that school leadership is also a practice that entails having people work in everyday contexts; make experiences; have norms, opinions, and values; listen to gurus and good advice; and exercise discretion. Furthermore, much of the research carried out is politically motivated and funded (e.g. as part of transnational educational reforms). The research is not controlled by the profession itself.

Thus, the knowledge base of school leadership remains contested and questionable. It is not unlike that of the established professions, but it seems more practical, normative, and politically defined. To a lesser extent, it is defined by the 'custodians' of the profession (i.e. the academics) and their criteria of logical consistency and rationality.

The notion of a 'knowledge dynamic' may be better at capturing the actual knowledge production in school leadership. It assumes a contestation of knowledge, and it allows practitioners to serve as reflexive users and co-producers of knowledge – not simply as implementors of standards. However, insisting on this notion does not necessarily lead to a goal of becoming a full-fledged profession. The term 'knowledge dynamic' may be too realistic or frank a description.

The notion of a knowledge base captures the functional use of academic knowledge taking place in the established professions; however, as pointed out, it is also a bulwark invented to legitimise power. The question for school leadership is what notion to stake on: the realistic or the persuasive? The frank or the power accruing?

Education and training

Another focal point for establishing a profession involves the competencies and skills acquired through education and training. These features insert a distinction between the professional and the layman. The point of departure for school leadership is a context in which a strong focus is placed on education and training, supplemented by a strong belief in the importance of leadership as measured by educational results.

The education and training of school leaders have existed for a long time and, especially in the past few decades, most countries have formalised educational programmes for future and current school leaders. A majority of school leaders have backgrounds as teachers, and most preparatory programmes admit on this background. Developing programmes are part-time, and they admit on the basis of an attained position as a school leader. Furthermore, a plethora of informal courses of varying lengths complement the formalised programmes. Together, these programmes constitute clear support for the development of a profession.

This development points in several directions in terms of the aim and content of the educational programmes. On the one hand, we observe the development of an orthodoxy focused on technical skills, efficiency, and improvement of standardised test scores. This orthodoxy, or paradigm, of school leadership was mentioned above, and it includes efforts to develop standards which school leaders must follow and to which the educational programmes are organised. On the other hand, we observe so-called heterodoxies who reinterpret ideas of 'improvement', 'effectiveness', and 'standards' as losses of autonomy, agency, and discretion that ultimately lead to a process of deprofessionalisation.

Recruitment and control of the selection, training, and entrance of candidates is not decided solely by the occupation. To a great extent, it is decided politically. Consequently, a rather low standard has been observed among candidates for years. This might impair the ambitions of becoming a profession.

Ethics

Professional ethics is closely connected to values such as care, altruism, client orientation, and service – in short, values expressing virtues. This applies to Talcott Parsons, who distinguished the professional from the businessman based on these types of values. The professional was primarily oriented towards service, while the businessman was primarily oriented towards money. Today, codes of ethics developed by associations of school leaders still express similar values, but a difference seems to exist between the Nordic and Anglo-Saxon countries in terms of how clearly these values are distinguished from other goals directed at the school (e.g. meeting standards and delivering results). In the Nordic countries, values are clearly distinguished from instrumental goals. In Anglo-Saxon countries, altruistic values and instrumental goals appear side by side *as* values.

Codes of ethics have been developed or are well underway in Anglo-Saxon countries, as well as in the Nordic countries. In the Nordic countries, ethics tends to be a limited theme in a more general professionalisation strategy. By contrast, the British Association of School and College Leaders (ASCL) has developed a specific framework describing seven principles of ethical leadership in education. Some research has described, for example, the tension that may arise between following ethical values and delivering results. However, compared with the previous themes on knowledge bases and education, we assess the volume of this research to be smaller. This might reflect the relative strength and amount of attention these themes enjoy, with knowledge and education getting the upper hand.

While the codes of ethics seem to be well developed, ethical awareness and praxis seem more limited. Thus, school leaders can possibly perceive themselves as ethical if they know and can reiterate the code of ethics, while in fact acting unethically in praxis. We have given some examples of this involving school leaders who do not reflect on and consider the wants of the teachers who are their responsibility. More specifically, we point to leaders who expose vulnerable and confidential information about teachers in leader networks. These examples show some of the ethical paradoxes and dilemmas which the attempt to professionalise school leadership must take into consideration. If not taken into account, they can lead to ethical pressure that is understood as the inability to live up to personal and professional values.

Working conditions

The process of professionalisation depends on the frameworks that offer possibilities and constraints regarding school leaders' daily practices. In most countries and educational systems, these frameworks have undergone remarkable changes involving new relations with the governing authorities, as well as new relations between schools. In general, we observe a tendency towards less detailed regulation of the single school. Schools and leaders have gained more autonomy in a more competitive environment. In return, they have gained more refined audit systems, whereby schools can be measured and compared through a spectrum of indicators. We have argued that the achieved autonomy depends on the results of the schools: schools with better results have more autonomy, while schools with worse results have less autonomy and more inspections.

School leaders' (lack of) possibilities to act in these frameworks are important for the realisation of a professionalisation project. As illustrated by a current reform of basic school in Denmark, school leaders have obtained a new portfolio of tasks – namely, finance and strategy. At the same time, school leaders are expected to perform the usual tasks and, to a greater extent than before, intervene in teachers' work. In many cases, the pressure to deliver results can limit school leaders' possibilities for making independent decisions based on their professional judgement. The newly gained autonomy is also limited or hindered by actors who assess the occupation using nonprofessional criteria. Generally, these limitations contradict the attempt to become a profession.

The changed environment and new tasks lead to new decisions, which have consequences for students. Focus on results may neglect other purposes of the school. On a macro level, the strengthened competition between schools seems to entail the success of some schools and the failure of others. In other words, competition is a zero-sum game. Striving to obtain the 'best' students (i.e. the academically most able students) involves ethical stances which a process of professionalisation may qualify and support.

Some claim that school leaders have not obtained the power necessary to resolve the responsibilities assigned to them – for instance, to hire and fire teachers. A separation from their original profession as teachers seems to be a consequence of, and prerequisite for, establishing school leadership as a profession. We will discuss whether this is so in the next section on the formation of a professional identity.

Formation of a professional identity

What identities are made possible in connection to professionalisation, what identities become more difficult to pursue, and are school leaders bound by a sense of shared identity? In investigating these questions, we have relied on existing research, as well as examples from our own research.

Some research has been conducted on this topic, but it is not comparable to that conducted on the knowledge base and education. We have organised the existing research into the following three subthemes: (1) studies on the dilemmas and problems school leaders may face in the intersection between welfare systems and New Public Management, (2) studies on 'new' leader identities crafted in private/corporate schools, and (3) studies preoccupied with conceptualising the idea of a professional identity. Much of this research is based on interview data, which is often analysed from narrative perspectives that show identity in the making – that is, identity as an open, discursive, social, and sensemaking construct.

Our own research is based on a similar approach. Thus, we have given three examples of school leaders narrating their professional identities. These narratives are told along the lines of a fairy tale, usually with the school leader in a starring role, modernising or turning around a school which has had some problems. They seem to fall into a continuum representing the following identities: the first among equals, the leader in between, and the generic leader.

We find the generic leader to be the most plausible under the current conditions. He or she seems to best match today's recruitment systems, education and training programmes, and expectations in practice. The first among equals, who has a long experience as teacher, a bumpy way to the top, and little or no formal education and training, seems to be on the way out in the Danish school system. This was also illustrated in Chapter 6, where a retired school inspector was quoted for saying, 'There will never be one like me again'.

However, whether this generic leader who does not necessarily have a background as a teacher will also turn out to be the professional school leader remains uncertain. This is a struggle which, among other things, depends on the developments in the other areas of the overall professionalisation project. Staying close to teachers and pupils, rather than generalising and pulling leaders towards each other and the external world, is a quality stressed by many. Being bound by a sense of shared identity is not advocated by all – if that identity glosses over teachers, pupils, or other relevant stakeholders in the school.

Conclusion

Drawing an unequivocal conclusion regarding the professionalisation of school leadership is difficult. As described, the development of this occupation is not identical in all the areas analysed, and efforts are not integrated. Knowledge and education are areas of investment, while ethics, working conditions, and identity are less noticed areas. Moreover, the development of each of these areas entails more than a single process from A to B and, in fact, involves multiple processes. This is due to contestation: the actors do not agree on a path to follow but tend to pull in different directions.

Nevertheless, we can observe development and efforts in all areas. On this basis, we conclude that professionalisation of school leadership is taking place, but not to the extent that school leadership is now a full-fledged profession. Rather, it is an emerging profession similar to other and previous semi-professions. When embarking on this project, we assumed this to be the case, but we now have a better understanding of how this is so.

Having observed the discrepancy and multiple processes occurring in school leadership as a field, we consider whether not one but two professionalisation projects are unfolding. One of these emphasises technical knowledge, standards, and delivery of results, and the other emphasises values, ethics, and the ability to exercise discretion. This would explain why the two positions we have referred to as orthodoxies and heterodoxies can disagree so fundamentally on what a process of professionalisation entails. To the orthodoxies, the 'technical' process entails professionalisation, whereas, to the heterodoxies, it entails deprofessionalisation. Conversely, to the heterodoxies, the 'value' approach entails professionalisation, while to the orthodoxies, it entails deprofessionalisation or something unqualified, ineffective, and unfounded.

This disagreement between heterodoxies and orthodoxies is, however, consistent with the internal disagreement displayed by the early and elder

Talcott Parsons. Therefore, it may be understood as a tension necessary to the professionalisation of school leadership.

Implications of becoming a profession

The endeavour to become a profession has some advantages and disadvantages, which we have only indicated in this book. Our purpose has not been to side for or against professionalisation, but to analyse the efforts already taking place. Still, we will briefly point to some of the advantages and disadvantages at the end of our contribution. In this way, we hope to contribute to the discussion on the future development of school leadership as an occupation. It is not certain, natural, or necessarily sensible that school leadership should pursue a path of further professionalisation. There are advantages and disadvantages to this, as we will point out, and the result is dependent on the specific nature of the professionalisation project – be it technical, values-based, or otherwise.

From school leaders' perspective, an obvious advantage of becoming a profession is the fact that they gain further legitimacy and power vis-à-vis the surrounding environment. It allows them to act and talk with greater impact, and it might allow them to wrest some of the political control characterising the field. Furthermore, a high degree of professionalism can make school leaders better at their job. This is important when new and complex tasks are taken into consideration. Skills and competencies are necessary to fulfil these tasks, be they technical, personal, analytical, reflective, or normative. Another advantage is the shared community, which can help create a new vocabulary and new work identities. Also, a shared community can perform collegiate control, as well as mitigate some of the loneliness and vulnerability associated with being a school leader.

A disadvantage of being a profession is the closedness and absolute power which can occur in relation to clients and to parallel and subordinate professions (e.g. teachers). An example of this is when a school leader demands a teacher to 'get off the bus' if that teacher does not agree with the direction taken. The same tendency can be discerned from 'generic leadership'. Here, leaders tend to forget their backgrounds as teachers, purposes specific to schools, and that they are school leaders. Instead, they develop a secret language, secluded (generic) identities, goals known mostly to themselves, and grandiose ideas of managing schools by themselves.

What path school leadership will follow, and what the consequences will be, can only the future tell. With this contribution, we have attempted to illuminate some possible lines of development that school leaders, professional associations, and politicians may take into consideration.

References

Abbott, A. (1988). *The system of professions.* The University of Chicago Press.
Abbott, A. (2005). Linked ecologies: States and universities as environments for professions. *Sociological Theory, 23*(3), 245–274. https://doi.org/10.1111/j.0735-2751.2005.00253.x
Ackroyd, S., Kirkpatrick, I., & Walker, R. M. (2007). Public management reform in the UK and its consequences for professional organization: A comparative analysis. *Public Administration, 85*(1), 9–26. https://doi.org/10.1111/j.1467-9299.2007.00631.x
Adamowski, S., Therriault, S. B., & Cavanna, A. P. (2007). *The autonomy gap: Barriers to effective school leadership.* American Institutes for Research and Thomas B. Fordham Institute.
Alexandrou, A., & Swaffield, S. (2012). Teacher leadership and professional development: Perspectives, connections and prospects. *Professional Development in Education, 38*(2), 159–167. https://doi.org/10.1080/19415257.2012.657557
Alexandrou, A., & Swaffield, S. (2014). *Teacher leadership and professional development.* New York: Routledge.
Alvesson, M., Blom, M., & Sveningsson, S. (2017). *Reflexive leadership: Organising in an imperfect world.* London: Sage.
Alvesson, M., & Willmott, H. (2002). Identity regulation as organizational control: Producing the appropriate individual. *Journal of Management Studies, 39*(5), 619. https://doi.org/10.1111/1467-6486.00305
Ärlestig, H., Day, C., & Johansson, O. (Eds.) (2016). *A decade of research on school principals.* Cham: Springer.
Association of School and College Leaders (2018). *Navigating the educational moral maze.* Retrieved from: www.ascl.org.uk/ASCL/media/ASCL/Our%20view/Campaigns/Navigating-the-educational-moral-maze.pdf
Augier, M., & March, J. (2011). *The roots, rituals, and rhetorics of change: North American business schools after the Second World War.* Stanford University Press.
Avolio, B. J. (2010). Pursuing authentic leadership development. In: N. Nohria & R. Khurana (Eds.), *Handbook of leadership theory and practice: Pursuing authentic leadership development.* Boston, MA: Harvard Business Press.
Avolio, B. J., & Gardner, W. L. (2005). Authentic leadership development: Getting to the root of positive forms of leadership. *The Leadership Quarterly, 16*(3), 315–338. https://doi.org/10.1016/j.leaqua.2005.03.001

References

Ball, S. J. (1994). *Education reform: A critical and post-structural approach*. Buckingham: Open University Press.

Bass, B. M. (1990). From transactional to transformational leadership: Learning to share the vision. *Organizational Dynamics, 18*(3), 19–31. https://doi.org/10.1016/0090-2616(90)90061-S

Bezzina, M. (2012). Paying attention to moral purpose in leading learning: Lessons from the Leaders Transforming Learning and Learners Project. *Educational Management Administration & Leadership, 40*(2), 248–271. https://doi.org/10.1177/1741143211427979

Bjørnholt B., Mikkelsen, M. F., Kjer, M. G., Flyger, C. I., Kjaergaard, L., Wagner, M. R., Andersen, M., & Wellsandt, K. (2019). *Skoleledelse under folkeskolereformen* [School leadership under the reform of the basic school]. Rapport. København: Vibe – Det Nationale Forsknings- og Analysecenter for Velfærd.

Bjørnholt, B., Mikkelsen, M. F., & Tranholm, E. (2018). *Skoleledernes oplevelser af folkeskolen i folkeskolereformens fjerde år. En kortlægning* [School leaders' experiences of the basic school after the fourth year of the reform]. Rapport. København: VIVE – Det Nationale Forsknings- og Analysecenter for Velfærd.

Bourdieu, P. (1988). *Homo academicus*. Stanford University Press.

Bourdieu, P. (1996). *The state nobility. Elite schools in the field of power*. Stanford, CA: Stanford University Press.

Brante, T., Johnsson, E., Olofsson, G., & Svensson, L. G. (2015). *Professionerna i kundskabssamhällat* [The professions in the knowledge society]. Lund: Liber.

Brundrett, M., & Fitzgerald, T. (2007). The creation of national programmes of school leadership development in England and New Zealand: A comparative study. *School of Education Journal Articles*, Paper 8.

Burns, J. M. (1978). *Leadership*. Harper & Row.

Burrell, G., & Morgan, G. (1979). *Sociological paradigms and organisational analysis: Elements of the sociology of corporate life*. London: Heinemann Educational.

Bush, T., & Glover, D. (2003). *School leadership: Concepts and evidence*. National College for School Leadership.

Bøje, J. D. (2017). Profession og pædagogik [Profession and pedagogy]. In: J. Dolin, G. H. Ingerslev, & H. S. Jørgensen (Eds.), *Gymnasiepædagogik. En grundbog*. København: Hans Reitzels Forlag.

Bøje, J. D. (2020). En skoleleder skal også ud med skrald og tørre bordene af. Skoleledelse mellem profan hverdagspraksis, magisk management og religiøst lederskab [A school leader must also carry out rubbish and wipe off the tables: School leadership between profane practice, magical management, and religious leadership]. *Tidsskrift for Professionsstudier, 16*(30), 93–101.

Bøje, J. D., & Frederiksen, L. F. (2019). Leaders of the profession and professional leaders: School leaders making sense of themselves and their job. *International Journal of Leadership in Education, 24*(3), 291–312. https://doi.org/10.1080/13603124.2019.1591515

Børne- og Ungeministeriet (2020). *Bekendtgørelse af lov om folkeskolen* [Departemental order of the law on the basic school]. Børne- og ungeministeriet.

Camic, C. (1992). Structure after 50 years: The anatomy of a charter. In: P. Hamilton (Ed.), *Talcott Parsons: Critical assessments, volume 1*. London: Routledge.

References

Carlgren, I. (1990). Tyst kunskap och frågan om praktikkens förändring. Några funderingar utifrån forskningen om lärarkunskap [Tacit knowledge and the question of change in practices: Some thoughts on research on teacher knowledge]. *Nordisk Pedagogik*, *3*, 167–172.

Cherkowski, S., Walker, K. D., & Kutsyuruba, B. (2015). Principals' moral agency and ethical decision-making: Toward a transformational ethics. *International Journal of Education Policy and Leadership*, *10*(5), 1–17.

Christ, C., & Dobbins, M. (2016). Increasing school autonomy in Western Europe: A comparative analysis of its causes and forms. *European Societies*, *18*(4), 359–388. https://doi.org/10.1080/14616696.2016.1172716

Clark, T., & Salaman, G. (1996). The management guru as organizational witchdoctor. *Organization*, *3*(1), 85–107. https://doi.org/10.1177/135050849631005

Collins, D. (2005). Pyramid schemes and programmatic management: Critical reflections on the 'Guru Industry'. *Culture and Organization*, *11*(1), 33–44. https://doi.org/10.1080/14759550500062318

Conger, J. A. (1998). Qualitative research as the cornerstone methodology for understanding leadership. *The Leadership Quarterly*, *9*(1), 107–121.

Cottrell, M., & James, C. (2016). Theorizing headteacher socialization from a role boundary perspective. *Educational Management Administration & Leadership*, *44*(1), 6–19. https://doi.org/10.1177/1741143214549976

Courtney, S. J. (2016). Corporatising school leadership through hysteresis. *British Journal of Sociology of Education*, *38*(7), 1054–1067. https://doi.org/10.1080/01425692.2016.1245131

Courtney, S. J., & Gunter, H. M. (2015). Get off my bus! School leaders, vision work and the elimination of teachers. *International Journal of Leadership in Education*, *18*(4), 395–417. https://doi.org/10.1080/13603124.2014.992476

Cranston, N. (2013). School leaders leading: Professional responsibility not accountability as the key focus. *Educational Management Administration and Leadership*, *41*(2), 129–142. https://doi.org/10.1177/1741143212468348

Crawford, M. (2012). Solo and distributed leadership: Definitions and dilemmas. *Educational Management Administration & Leadership*, *40*(5), 610–620. https://doi.org/10.1177/1741143212451175

Creighton, T. (2002). Standards for education administration preparation programs: Okay, but don't we have the cart before the horse? *Journal of School Leadership*, *12*, 526–550. https://doi.org/10.1177/105268460201200504

Crow, G. M., Day, C., & Møller, J. (2017). Framing research on school principals' identities. *International Journal of Leadership in Education*, *20*(3), 265–277. https://doi.org/10.1080/13603124.2015.1123299

Crow, G. M., & Whiteman, R. S. (2016). Effective preparation program features: A literature review. *Journal of Research on Leadership Education*, *11*(1), 120–148. https://doi.org/10.1177/1942775116634694

Cruz Martins, S. D., Capucha, L., & Sebastião, J. (Eds.) (2019). *School autonomy, organization and performance in Europe. A comparative analysis for the period from 2000 to 2015*. Lisbon: Centre for Research and Studies in Sociology (CIES).

Cubberley, E. P. (1929). *Public school administration*. Houghton Mifflin Company.

Culbertson, J. A. (1981). Antecedents of the theory movement. *Educational Administration Quarterly, 17*(1), 25–47. https://doi.org/10.1177/0013161X8101700103

Czarniawska, B. (1998). *A narrative approach to organization studies.* Thousand Oaks, CA: Sage.

Darling-Hammond, L., Meyerson, D., LaPointe, M., & Orr, M. T. (2010). *Preparing principals for a changing world: Lessons from effective school leadership programs.* John Wiley and Sons Ltd.

Darling-Hammond, L., & Rothman, R. (2011). *Teacher and leader effectiveness in high performing education systems.* Stanford Center for Opportunity Policy in Education.

Day, C., & Sammons, P. (2016). *Successful school leadership.* Education Development Trust.

Derrington, M. L., & Larsen, D. E. (2012). Principal pressure in the middle of accountability. *Journal of Cases in Educational Leadership, 15*(4), 65–75. https://doi.org/10.1177/1555458912470656

Dewey, J. (2011/1916). *Democracy and education.* Simon & Brown.

Duignan, P. A. (2014). Authenticity in educational leadership: History, ideal, reality. *Journal of Educational Administration, 52*(2), 152–172. https://doi.org/10.1108/JEA-01-2014-0012

Durkheim, E. (1957). *Professional ethics and civil morals.* The Free Press.

Durkheim, E. (1984). *The division of labor in society.* The Free Press.

Dutton, S. (1903). *School management: Practical suggestions concerning the conduct and life of the school.* C. Scribner & Sons.

Eacott, S. (2011). Preparing 'educational' leaders in managerialist times: An Australian story. *Journal of Educational Administration and History, 43*(1), 43–59. https://doi.org/10.1080/00220620.2010.532865

English, F. W. (2000). Pssssst! What does one call a set of non-empirical beliefs required to be accepted on faith and enforced by authority? [Answer: A religion, AKA the ISLLC standards]. *International Journal of Leadership in Education, 3*(2), 159–167. https://doi.org/10.1080/136031200292803

English, F. W. (2002). The point of scientificity, the fall of the epistemological dominos, and the end of the field of educational administration. *Studies in Philosophy & Education, 21*(2), 109–136. https://doi.org/10.1023/A:1014432804622

English, F. W. (2006). The unintended consequences of standardized knowledge base in advancing educational leadership preparation. *Educational Administration Quarterly, 42*(3), 461–472. https://doi.org/10.1177/0013161X06289675

Eriksen, T., & Jørgensen, A. M. (2005). *Professionsidentitet i forandring* [Professional identity in change]. København: Akademisk Forlag.

Etzioni, A. (Ed.) (1969). *The semi-professions and their organization.* The Free Press.

Evetts, J. (2003). The sociological analysis of professionalism: Occupational change in the modern world. *International Sociology, 18*(2), 395–415. https://doi.org/10.1177/0268580903018002005

Evetts, J. (2011). A new professionalism? Challenges and opportunities. *Current Sociology, 59*(49), 406–422. https://doi.org/10.1177/0011392111402585

Fournier, V. (1999). The appeal to 'professionalism' as a disciplinary mechanism. *The Sociological Review, 47*(2), 280–307. https://doi.org/10.1111/1467-954X.00173

References

Freidson, E. (2001). *Professionalism, the third logic: On the practice of knowledge*. Polity.

Fuller, K. (2012). Leading with emancipatory intent: Headteachers' approaches to pupil diversity. *Educational Management Administration & Leadership*, 40(6), 672–689. https://doi.org/10.1177/1741143212456911

Gavino, J. C., & Portugal, E. J. (2013). Leadership framework: A preliminary qualitative research using the Critical Incident method. *World Review of Business Research*, 3(4), 40–52.

Goldspink, C. (2007). Rethinking educational reform: A loosely coupled and complex systems perspective. *Educational Management Administration & Leadership*, 35(1), 27–50. https://doi.org/10.1177/1741143207068219

Goode, W. J. (1957). Community within a community: The professions. *American Sociological Review*, 22(2), 194–200. https://doi.org/10.2307/2088857

Goodson, I. (2000). The principled professional. *Prospects*, 30(2), 181–188. https://doi.org/10.1007/BF02754064

Goodson, I. (2008). *Investigating teacher's life and work*. Sense Publishers.

Greenfield, T. B. (1986). The decline and fall of science in educational administration. *Interchange*, 17(2), 57–80. https://doi.org/10.1007/BF01807469

Greenfield, T. B., & Ribbins, P. (1993). *Greenfield on educational administration: Towards a humane craft*. London: Routledge.

Greimas, A. J. (1973). Actants, actors, and figures on meaning: Selected writings in semiotic theory. *Theory and History of Literature*, 38, 106–120.

Grimen, H., & Molander, A. (2008). Profesjon og skjønn [Profession and discretion]. In: A. Molander & L. I. Terum (Eds.), *Profesjonsstudier*. Oslo: Universitetsforlaget.

Gronn, P. (1999). *The making of educational leaders*. London: Cassell.

Gronn, P. (2002). Designer leadership: The emerging global adoption of preparation standards. *Journal of School Leadership*, 12, 552–578. https://doi.org/10.1177/105268460201200505

Gronn, P. (2003). *The new work of educational leaders: Changing leadership practice in an era of school reform*. London: Paul Chapman.

Gunter, H. (2016). Intellectual histories of school leadership: Implications for professional preparation. *Acta Didactica Norge*, 10(4), 27–47. https://doi.org/10.5617/adno.3988

Gunter, H., & Forrester, G. (2009). School leadership and education policymaking in England. *Policy Studies*, 30(5), 495–511. https://doi.org/10.1080/01442870902899947

Gunter, H., & Ribbins, P. (2003). The field of educational leadership: Studying maps and mapping studies. *British Journal of Educational Studies*, 51(3), 254–281. https://doi.org/10.1111/1467-8527.t01-1-00238

Hagedorn-Rasmussen, P., & Klethagen, P. (2019). International management concepts meeting Nordic working life. In: H. Hvid & E. Falkum (Eds.), *Work and wellbeing in the nordic countries: Critical perspectives on the world's best working lives*. New York: Routledge.

Hall, L. (2016). *Ledelse og læringsudbytte: Tre skoleledelsesformer* [Leadership and learning outcomes: Three reforms]. Frederiksberg: Samfundslitteratur.

References

Hallinger, P. (2005). Instructional leadership and the school principal: A passing fancy that refuses to fade away. *Leadership and Policy in Schools*, *4*(3), 221–239. https://doi.org/10.1080/15700760500244793

Hallinger, P. (2013). A conceptual framework for systematic reviews of research in educational leadership and management. *Journal of Educational Administration*, *51*(2), 126–149. https://doi.org/10.1108/09578231311304670

Hamilton, P. (1992). General commentary. In: P. Hamilton (Ed.), *Talcott Parsons: Critical assessments, volume 1*. London: Routledge.

Hammersley-Fletcher, L., Kilicoglu, D., & Kilicoglu, G. (2020). Does autonomy exist? Comparing the autonomy of teachers and senior leaders in England and Turkey. *Oxford Review of Education*, *47*(2), 189–206. https://doi:10.1080/0305 4985.2020.1824900

Hansen, D. R., & Bøje, J. D. (2017). The 'strong' state and the 'soft' market in educational reform processes: Management philosophies and their consequences. *Power & Education*, *9*(1), 18–36. https://doi.org/10.1177/1757743817692600

Hansen, D. R., & Frederiksen, L. F. (2017). The 'crucified' leader: Cynicism, fantasies and paradoxes in education. *Studies in Philosophy and Education*, *36*(4), 425–444. https://doi.org/10.1007/s11217-016-9539-y

Hargreaves, A., & Fullan, A. (2012). *Professional capital*. London: Routledge.

Hargreaves, D. H. (1996). *Teaching as a research-based profession, possibilities and prospects*. Teacher Training Agency Annual Lecture. Teacher Training Agency.

Harris, A. (2005). Leading from the chalk-face: An overview of school leadership. *Leadership*, *1*(1), 73–87. https://doi.org/10.1177/1742715005049352

Harris, A. (2008). *Distributed school leadership: Developing tomorrow's leaders*. Routledge.

Hartley, D. (2010). Paradigms: How far does research in distributed leadership 'stretch'? *Educational Management Administration & Leadership*, *38*(3), 271–285. https://doi.org/10.1177/1741143209359716

Heffernan, A. (2018). Power and the 'autonomous' principal: Autonomy, teacher development, and school leaders' work, *Journal of Educational Administration and History*, *50*(4), 379–396. https://doi.org/10.1080/00220620.2018.1518318

Heggen, K. (2008). Profesjon og identitet [Profession and identity]. In: A. Molander og L. I. Terum: *Profesjonsstudier* [Studies of professions]. Oslo: Universitetsforlaget.

Hein, H. H. (2009). Kunsten at lede primadonnaer [The art of leading prima donnas]. *Peripeti*, *12*, 79–90.

Hightower, B. B., & Klinker, J. A. F. (2012). When ethics and policy collide. *Journal of Cases in Educational Leadership*, *15*(2), 103–111. https://doi.org/10.1177/1555458911413888

Hildebrandt, S. (2017). Vanvittig fælles uddannelse for alle skoleledere [Crazy common education of all school leaders]. *Mandag Morgen*, blog nr. 23.

Hinkin, T. R., & Tracey, J. B. (1999). The relevance of charisma for transformational leadership in stable organizations. *Journal of Organizational Change Management*, *12*(2), 105–119. https://doi.org/10.1108/09534819910263659

Hjort, K. (2005). *Professionaliseringen i den offentlige sektor* [Professionalisation in the public sector]. Roskilde Universitetsforlag.

References

Hjort, K., & Aili, C. (2010). Prioriteringskompetens: Konkurrerande välfärdsprincipper och nya krav på lärarprofessionen [The competence of prioritisation: Competing welfare principles and new requirements of the teaching profession]. In: G. Brante och K. Hjort: *Dilemman i skolan: Aktuelle utmaninger och professionella omställingar* [The dilemma in school: Current challenges and professional changes]. Kristianstad: Kristianstad University Press, pp. 8–25.

Hjort, K., Bøje, J. D., Raae, P. H., Ribers, B., & Stanek, A. (2018). *En god (nok) leder. Professionalisering af skoleledelse [A good (enough) leader: Professionalisation of school leadership]*. København: Werkstatt.

Hood, C. (1991). A public management for all seasons? *Public Administration*, 69(1), 3–19. https://doi.org/10.1111/j.1467-9299.1991.tb00779.x

House, R. (1976). *A 1976 theory of charismatic leadership*. Working Paper Series 76–06. Toronto University.

Jacobsen, A. J., & Buch, A. (2016). Management of professionals in school practices. *Professions & Professionalism*, 6(3), 1–16. https://doi.org/10.7577/pp.1503

Johnson, T. (1972). *Professions and power*. London: Macmillan.

Karlsen, M. P., & Villadsen, K. (2013). Når ledelsen ler med: Om forholdet mellem magt og humor i samtidens ledelse [When leaders join the laughing: On the relationship between power and humor in contemporary leadership]. *Nordiske Organisasjonsstudier*, 15(1), 55–77.

Keddie, A. (2014). 'It's like Spiderman . . . with great power comes great responsibility': school autonomy, school context and the audit culture. *School Leadership & Management*, 34(5), 502–517. https:/doi.org/10.1080/13632434.2014.938040

Keddie, A. (2015). School autonomy, accountability and collaboration: A critical review. *Journal of Educational Administration and History*, 47(1), 1–17. https://doi.org/10.1080/00220620.2015.974146

Keddie, A. (2017). Primary school leadership in England: Performativity and matters of professionalism. *British Journal of Sociology of Education*, 38(8), 1245–1257. https://doi.org/10.1080/01425692.2016.1273758

Kelchtermans, G., Piot, L., & Ballet, K. (2011). The lucid loneliness of the gatekeeper: Exploring the emotional dimension in principals' work lives. *Oxford Review of Education*, 37(1), 93–108. https://doi.org/10.1080/03054985.2010.545192

Kimber, M., & Campbell, M. (2014). Exploring ethical dilemmas for principals arising from role conflict with school counsellors. *Educational Management Administration & Leadership*, 42(2), 207–225. https://doi.org/10.1177/1741143213499259

Kipping, M. (2011). Hollow from the start: Image professionalism in management consulting. *Current Sociology*, 59(4), 530–550. https://doi.org/10.1177/0011392111402727

Kjer, M. G., Baviskar, S., & Winter, S. C. (2015). *Skoleledelse i folkeskolereformens første år. En kortlægning* [School leadership in the first year of the reform of the basic school: A mapping]. SFI – Det Nationale Forskningscenter for Velfærd.

Kjer, M. G., & Jensen, V. M. (2018). *Styring, autonomi og pædagogisk ledelse af folkeskolerne under reformen* [Governance, autonomy and pedagogical leadership of the basic school during the reform]. København: VIVE – Det Nationale Forsknings- og Analysecenter for Velfærd.

References

Kjer, M. G., & Rosdahl, A. (2016). *Ledelse af forandringer i folkeskolen* [Leadership of change in the basic school]. København: SFI – Det Nationale Forskningscenter for Velfærd.

Klausen, K. K., Michelsen, J., & Nielsen, D. M. (2011). *Den decentrale leder* [The decentral leader]. Odense: Syddansk Universitet.

Kommunernes Landsforening (2017). *Grunduddannelse af skoleledere – fremtidige kompetencebehov og uddannelsestilbud* [Elementary education of school leaders; Future competences and educational provision]. Kommunernes Landsforening.

Larsen, B., & Hein, H. H. (eds.) (2007). *De nye professionelle* [The new professionals]. København: Jurist- og Økonomiforbundets Forlag.

Larson, M. S. (1977). *The rise of professionalism: A sociological analysis*. University of California Press.

Lederforeningen (2008). *Skoleledelse: En profession i sig selv.* [School leadership: A profession in itself]. Lederforeningen.

Leithwood, K., Jantzi, D., & Steinbach, R. (1999). *Changing leadership for changing times*. Philadelphia, PA: Open University Press.

Leithwood, K., Louis, K. S., Anderson, S., & Wahlstrom, K. (2004). *How leadership influences student learning: A review of research for the Learning from Leadership Project*. The Wallace Foundation.

Levacic, R. (2002). Efficiency, equity and autonomy. In: T. Bush & L. Bell (Eds.), *The principles and practice of educational management*. Paul Chapman Publishing.

Løgstrup, K. E. (1997/1956). *The ethical demand*. Notre Dame University Press.

Lortie, D. C. (1969). The balance of control and autonomy in elementary school teaching. In: A. Etzioni (Ed.), *The semi-professions and their organization*. The Free Press.

Lumby, J., Crow, G. M., & Pashiardis, P. (Eds.) (2008). *International handbook on the preparation and development of school leaders*. New York, NY: Routledge.

Lumby, J., & English, F. (2009). From simplicism to complexity in leadership identity and preparation: Exploring the lineage and dark secrets. *International Journal of Leadership in Education*, *12*(2), 98–114 https://doi.org/10.1080/13603120802449678

Male, T., & Palaiologou, I. (2012). Learning-centred leadership or pedagogical leadership? An alternative approach to leadership in education contexts. *International Journal of Leadership in Education*, *15*(1), 107–118. https://doi.org/10.1080/13603124.2011.617839

March, J. G. (1991). How decisions happen in organizations. *Human-Computer Interaction*, *6*(2), 95–117. https://doi.org/10.1207/s15327051hci0602_1

McCarthy, M. M., & Forsyth, P. B. (2009). An historical review of research and development activities pertaining to the preparation of school leaders. In: M. D. Young, G. M. Crow, J. Murphy, & R. T. Ogawa (Eds.), *Handbook of research on the education of school leaders*. New York, NY: Routledge.

McIntyre, K. E. (1966). *Selection of educational administrators*. University Council for Educational Administration.

Mik-Meyer, N. (2018). Organizational professionalism: Social workers negotiating tools of NPM. *Professions and Professionalism*, *8*(2), e2381. https://doi.org/10.7577/pp.2381

Millerson, G. (1964). *The qualifying associations: A study on professionalization.* Routledge & Paul.

Mintzberg, H. (2011). *Managing.* Pearson Education Limited.

Møller, J. (2016). Kvalifisering som skoleleder i en norsk kontekst: Et historisk tilbakeblikk og perspektiver på utdanning av skoleledere [Qualification of school leaders in a Norwegian context: A historical review and perspectives on education of school leaders]. *Acta Didactica Norge, 10*(4), 7–26. https://doi.org/10.5617/adno.3871

Moos, L. (Ed.) (2013). *Transnational influences on values and practices in Nordic educational leadership.* Dordrecht: Springer.

Moos, L. (2016). Denmark: Danish school leadership between welfare and competition. In: H. Ärlestig, C. Day, & O. Johansson (Eds.), *A decade of research on school principals.* Cham: Springer.

Moos, L. (2017). Neo-liberal governance leads education and educational leadership astray. In: M. Uljens, & R.M. Ylimaki (Eds.), *Bridging educational leadership, curriculum theory and didaktik: Non-affirmative theory of education.* Cham: Springer.

Moos, L., Carney, S., Johansson, O., & Mehlby, J. (2000). *Skoleledelse i Norden* [School leadership in the Nordic countries]. Nordisk Ministerråd.

Moos, L., Kofod, K., & Brinkkjær, U. (2011). *Rekruttering og fastholdelse af skoleledere* [Recruitment and retention of school leaders]. Århus: Danmarks Pædagogiske Universitetsskole.

Muel-Dreyfus, F. (2004). Uddannelse, jobforventninger og knuste drømme [Education, job expectations and shattered dreams]. In: K. A. Petersen (Ed.), *Praktikker i erhverv og uddannelse* [Practices in job and education.]. København: Frydenlund.

Murphy, J. (2005). Unpacking the foundations of ISLLC standards and addressing concerns in the academic community. *Educational Administration Quarterly, 41*(1), 154–191. https://doi.org/10.1177/0013161X04269580

Murphy, R. (1988). *Social closure: The theory of monopolization and exclusion.* Oxford: Clarendon Press.

Muzio, D., & Kirckpatrick, I. (2011). Introduction: Professions and organizations: A conceptual framework. *Current Sociology, 59*(4), 389–405. https://doi.org/10.1177/0011392111402584

National Policy Board for Educational Administration (2015). *Professional standards for educational leaders 2015.* Retrieved from: www.npbea.org

National Policy Board for Educational Administration (2018). *National Educational Leadership Preparation (NELP) program standards: Building level.* Retrieved from: www.npbea.org

Neeleman, A. (2019). The scope of school autonomy in practice: An empirically based classification of school interventions. *Journal of Educational Change, 20*(1), 31–55. https://doi.org/10.1007/s10833-018-9332-5

Nihlfors, E., & Johansson, O. (2013). *Rektor – en stark länk i styrningen av skolan* [Headmaster: A strong link in governance of schools]. Stockholm: SNS Förlag.

Noffke, S. E. (1997). Professional, personal, and political dimensions of action research. *Review of Research in Education, 22*, 305–343. https://doi.org/10.3102/0091732X022001305

References

Noordegraaf, M. (2011). Risky business: How professionals and professional fields (must) deal with organizational issues. *Organization, 32*(10), 1349–1371.

Oplatka, I. (2010). *The legacy of educational administration:. A historical analysis of an academic field*. Peter Lang GmbH.

Orr, M. T., & Orphanos, S. (2011). How graduate-level preparation influences the effectiveness of school leaders: A comparison of the outcomes of exemplary and conventional leadership preparation programs for principals. *Educational Administration Quarterly, 47*(1), 18–70. https://doi.org/10.1177/0011000010378610

Ottesen, E. (2016). Et kunnskapsgrunnlag for skoleledelse [A knowledge base for school leadership]. *Acta Didactica Norge, 10*(4), 69–81. https://doi.org/10.5617/adno.3923

Parkin, F. (1979). *Marxism and class theory: A bourgeois critique*. Tavistock Publications.

Parsons, T. (1951). *The social system*. The Free Press.

Parsons, T. (1954). The professions and social structure. In: T. Parsons (Ed.), *Essays in sociological theory*. The Free Press.

Parsons, T. (1968). Professions. In: D. Sills (Ed.), *International encyclopaedia of the social sciences, volume 12*. The Macmillan Company.

Pasgaard, N. J., & Malkenes, S. (2017). Norsk lederuddannelse er stik imod dansk tradition [Norwegian leadership education is contrary to Danish tradition]. *Skolemonitor*, November 21. Retrieved from: https://skoleliv.dk/debat/art6213815/Norsk-lederuddannelse-er-stik-imod-dansk-skoletradition?token=-76453651

Pounder, D. G. (2011). Leader preparation special issue: Implications for policy, practice, and research. *Educational Administration Quarterly, 47*(1), 258–267. https://doi.org/10.1177/0011000010378615

Propp, V. (1984). Theory and history of folklore. *Theory and History of Literature, 5*.

Pruzan, P. (2001). The question of organizational consciousness: Can organizations have values, virtues and visions? *Journal of Business Ethics, 29*(3), 271–284. https://doi.org/10.1023/A:1026577604845

Raae, P. H. (2008). *Rektor tænker organisation. Organisationsforestillinger i lyset af den dobbelte reform af det almene gymnasium* [Headmaster thinks organization: Organizational perceptions in the light of the double reform of the upper secondary school]. Gymnasiepædagogik Nr. 67. IFPR, Syddansk Universitet.

Raae, P. H. (2020). Effective leadership? A case study in work psychodynamics. In: H. S. Olesen (Ed.), *The societal unconscious: Psychosocial perspectives on adult learning*. Brill Sense.

Rayner, S. M. (2018). Leaders and leadership in a climate of uncertainty: A case study of structural change in England. *Educational Management Administration & Leadership, 46*(5), 749–763. https://doi.org/10.1177/1741143217707522

Rennisson, B. W. (2006). Selvskabt ledelse [Self-created leadership]. In: P. Helth (Ed.), *Lederskabelse – det personlige lederskab* [Leadership creation: The personal leadership]. København: Samfundslitteratur.

Rhoades, E. A. (2011). Literature reviews. *The Volta Review, 111*(3), 353–368.

Ribers, B. (2020). Ethical transformations: Developing ethical competencies for the social professions through action research. *European Journal of Social Work*. https://doi:10.1080/13691457.2020.1857704.

Ribers, B., Balslev, G., & Jensen, C. R. (2021). Education, collaboration and pedagogical phronesis: Essential dimensions in professional learning and development. *Professional Development in Education.* https://doi.org/10.1080/19415257.2021. 1902835

Riessman, C. K. (2017). Narrativ analyse i samfundsvidenskaberne [Narrative analysis in the social sciences]. In: M. Järvinen og N. Mik-Meyer: *Kvalitativ analyse. Syv traditioner* [Qualitative analysis: Seven traditions]. København: Hans Reitzels Forlag.

Risbøl, S. (2020). Den sidste skoleinspektør: Dialogen mellem skole og politikere er forsvundet [The last school inspector: The dialogue between school and politicians has disappeared]. *Skolemonitor,* October 22.

Roach, V., Smith, L. W., & Boutin, J. (2011). School leadership policy trends and developments: Policy expediency or policy excellence? *Educational Administration Quarterly, 47*(1), 71–113. https://doi.org/10.1177/0011000010378611

Robinson, V. (2011). *Student-centered leadership.* San Francisco: Jossey-Bass.

Rürup, M. (2007). *Innovationswege im deutschen Bildungssystem. Die Verbreitung der Idee ‚Schulautonomie' im Ländervergleich* [Innovation in German Educational System. The spread of the idea of school autonomy 'in a country comparison], Wiesbaden: VS Verlag.

Schön, D. A. (1983). *The reflective practitioner: How professionals think in action.* Basic Books.

Schön, D. A. (1987). *Educating the reflective practitioner.* San Fransisco: Jossey-Bass.

Scott, W. R. (2008). Lords of the dance: Professionals as institutional agents. *Organization Studies, 29*(2), 219–238. https://doi.org/10.1177/0170840607088151

Scribner, S. P., & Crow, G. M. (2012). Employing professional identities: Case study of a high school principal in a reform setting. *Leadership and Policy in Schools, 11*(3), 243–274. https://doi.org/10.1080/15700763.2012.654885

Simkins, T. (2012). Understanding school leadership and management development in England: Retrospect and prospect. *Educational Management, Administration & Leadership, 40*(5), 621–640. https://doi.org/10.1177/1741143212451172

Spicer, A., & Alvesson, M. (2011). *The metaphors we lead by.* London: Routledge.

Spillane, J. P. (2005). Distributed leadership. *The Educational Forum, 69*(2), 143–150. https://doi.org/10.1080/00131720508984678

Spillane, J. P. (2006). *Distributed leadership.* San Fransisco: Jossey-Bass.

Spillane, J. P., Halverson, R., & Diamond, J. (2001). *Towards a theory of leadership practice: A distributed perspective.* Working Article. Northwestern University, Institute for Policy Research.

Staunæs, D., Juelskjær, M., & Knudsen, H. (2009). Psy-ledelse. Nye former for (skole)ledelse set igennem tre optikker [Psy-leadership: New forms of (school) leadership viewed through three perspectives]. *Psyke & Logos, 30,* 510–532.

Tenuto, P. L., Gardiner, M. E., & Yamamoto, J. K. (2016). Leaders on the front line: Managing emotion for ethical decision making: A teaching case study for supervision of school personnel. *Journal of Cases in Educational Leadership, 19*(3), 11–26. https://doi.org/10.1177/1555458916657123

Tomlinson, M., O'Reilly, D., & Wallace, M. (2013). Developing leaders as symbolic violence: Reproducing public service leadership through the (misrecognized) development of leaders' capitals. *Management Learning, 44*(1), 81–97. https://doi.org/10.1177/1350507612472151

Uddannelses- og Forskningsministeriet (2020). *Godkendte udbydere af DOL pr. 1. april 2020* [Approved providers of DOL per. April 1, 2020]. Retrieved 08.10.2020 from: https://ufm.dk/uddannelse/videregaende-uddannelse/efter-og-videreuddannelse/certificering

Uljens, M., Møller, J., Ärlestig, H., & Frederiksen, L. F. (2013). The professionalization of Nordic school leadership. In: L. Moos (Ed.), *Transnational influences on values and practices in Nordic educational leadership: Is there a Nordic model?* Springer.

Uljens, M., & Ylimaki, R. M. (Eds.) (2017). *Bridging educational leadership, curriculum theory, and didaktik: Non-affirmative theory of education.* Cham: Springer.

Utdanningsforbundet (2017). *Utdanningsforbundets ledelsespolitikk.Rammevilkår for ledere* [Policy of leadership: Framework conditions]. Retrieved 28.05.2019 from: www.utdanningsforbundet.no/globalassets/medlemsgrupper/ledelse/lederoffensiven_ledelse–utdanningsforbundets-politikk.pdf

Væksthus for Ledelse (2008). *Kodeks for god ledelse – i kommuner og regioner* [Code of leadership: In municipalities and regions]. Væksthus for Ledelse.

Waring, J., & Currie, G. (2009). Managing expert knowledge: Organizational challenges and managerial futures for the UK medical profession. *Organization Studies, 30*(7), 755–778. https://doi.org/10.1177/0170840609104819

Weber, M. (1978). *Economy and society.* California University Press.

Weber, M. (2008/1921). Politics as a vocation. In: J. Dreimanis (Ed.), *Max Weber's complete writings on academic and political vocations.* Algora Publishing.

Weick, K. W. (1995). *Sensemaking in organizations.* Thousand Oaks, CA: Sage.

Weinberg, M., & Banks, S. (2019). Practising ethically in unethical times: Everyday resistance in social work. *Ethics and Social Welfare, 13*(4), 361–376. https://doi.org/10.1080/17496535.2019.1597141

Weinreich, E. (2014). *Hvilke offentlige ledere er der brug for når velfærdstænkningen flytter sig? Er diplomuddannelsens lederprofil svaret?* [What public leaders are needed when welfare thinking changes? Is the diploma program for leaders the answer?]. Ph.D.-afhandling ved. Copenhagen Business School.

Whitley, R. (2000). *The intellectual and social organization of the sciences.* Oxford University Press.

Wiedemann, F. (2019). *På kanten af ledelse. Analyser af konstruktive og destruktive ledelsesformer* [On the edge of leadership: Analyses of constructive and destructive forms of leadership]. Odense: Syddansk Universitetsforlag.

Wiedemann, F. (2021). Skoleledelse gennem tiden. Fra praktisk håndværker til forskningsinformeret læringsleder [School leadership through time: From practical craftsman to research-informed leader of learning]. *Tidsskrift for Professionsstudier, 32*(17), 38–49.

Wilensky, H. L. (1964). The professionalization of everyone? *American Journal of Sociology, 70*(2), 137–158. https://doi.org/10.1086/223790

Winter, S. (Ed.) (2017). *Gør skoleledelse en forskel? Ledelse af implementering af folkeskolereformen* [Does school leadership make a difference? Leading the implementation of the reform of basic school]. København: SFI – Det nationale Forskningscenter for Velfærd.

Witz, A. (1992). *Professions and patriarchy*. Routledge.

You, Y., & Morris, P. (2016). Imagining school autonomy in high-performing education systems: East Asia as a source of policy referencing in England. *Compare: A Journal of Comparative and International Education, 46*(6), 882–905. https://doi.org/10.1080/03057925.2015.1080115

Young, M. D., & Brewer, C. (2008). Fear and the preparation of school leaders: The role of ambiguity, anxiety, and power in meaning making. *Educational Policy, 22*(1), 106–129. https://doi.org/10.1177/0895904807311299

Young, M. D., Crow, G. M., Murphy, J., & Ogawa, R. T. (2009). *Handbook of research on the education of school leaders*. New York: Routledge.

Yukl, G. (1999). An evaluation of conceptual weaknesses in transformational and charismatic leadership theories. *Leadership Quarterly, 10*(2), 285–305. https://doi.org/10.1016/S1048-9843(99)00013-2

Zhang, W., & Brundrett, M. (2010). School leaders' perspectives on leadership learning: The case for informal and experiential learning. *Management in Education, 24*(4), 154–158. https://doi.org/10.1177/0892020610376792

Ziman, J. (1994). *Prometheus bound: Science in a dynamic steady state*. Cambridge University Press.

Index

Abbott, A. 2, 16, 21, 35
accountability 2–4, 27, 54, 69, 70–73
actantial model 85–86
ambiguity 80–82
Association of School and College Leaders 1, 55, 100
audit 46, 67, 101
autonomy 2–4, 11–14, 46, 56, 71, 101; definition 67; index 69
Avolio, B.J. 58–59

Banks, S. 57
Bezzina, M. 58, 64
Bourdieu, P. 15, 24–26, 44, 84
Brante, T. 12, 18
bureaucracy 12, 18, 27

Christ, C. 67, 73
client 8–9, 14, 17, 35, 67, 100
coaching 39, 58, 62
code of ethics 2, 53–54, 60
community within a community 10, 51, 78
competency 18, 63
competition 33, 63, 71–73, 98, 102
Courtney, S.J. 80, 83, 89
Cranston, N. 2
Creighton, T. 44–45
Crow, G.M. 38–39, 44, 80–81
Cruz Martins, S.D. 69
Czarniawska, B. 86, 94

Darling-Hammond, L. 2, 39, 81, 97
decentralisation 68, 70
decision: making 57, 66, 81; power 70; theory 72

deprofessionalisation 32, 46, 51
Dewey, J. 72
discipline 9, 21, 24–26, 30–34, 83
discretion 2, 12, 34, 49, 72, 99
Dobbins, M. 67, 73
Duignan, P.A. 58–59
Durkheim, E. 7–8, 18

Eacott, S. 2, 47, 83–84
effect 28–29, 31, 37, 40, 56
English, F.W. 23–24, 31–32, 35–36, 81–82
ethical: awareness 53; dilemma 61; practice 65; pressure 65; reflection 60
ethos 8, 14, 18, 53
Evetts, J. 2, 17

field 17, 21–36, 38–47, 80
first among equals 85–86, 97
Friedson, E. 16
functional approach 8

generic 32–33, 43, 49, 85
Goode, W.J. 7, 10, 51, 78–79
Goodson, I. 53, 89
Greimas, A.J. 85, 87
Grimen, H. 22, 34, 49, 72
Gronn, P. 28–29, 32–33, 78, 84
Gunter, H. 2, 24–27, 36, 39, 46–47, 83

habitus 47, 80
Hallinger, P. 29, 38
Hargreaves, D.H. 22–23, 32, 35
Harris, A. 27–29, 49, 58
heterodoxies 6, 38–46, 51, 100

Hjort, K. 1, 18, 34, 54, 61–65
hysteresis 80

identity 2, 10, 38, 79
inspection 47, 67, 73
Interstate School Leaders Licensure Consortium 30, 42

jurisdictional claim 16, 21–22, 35

Keddie, A. 2, 71, 74
Kelchtermans, G. 81, 84
knowledge: abstract 9, 14, 35–36; academic 22, 34–35, 43; base 21; dynamic 31, 36

leaderisation 46–48
leadership: charismatic 28; distributed 28–29, 53; instructional 27; interpretive 27, 49; transformational 27–28
Lederforeningen 1, 33, 54
Leithwood, K. 2, 27–28, 81, 97
Lortie, D. 11, 45
Lumby, J. 40, 81
Løgstrup, K.E. 54, 62

March, J.G. 43, 72
market 2, 16–19, 32, 43, 59
Millerson, G. 2, 7, 10–11
Mintzberg, H. 43
Molander, A. 22, 34, 49, 72
Møller, J. 34, 50
Moos, L. 2, 33–34, 48, 55, 82
moral distress 63–64
Murphy, J. 30–32

narrative 79–85
National Educational Leadership Preparation 42
National Policy Board for Educational Administration 30
Neeleman, A. 66, 68–70
Neo-Weberians 14
New Public Management 2, 18, 34, 57, 67, 71

OECD 68–70
Ofsted 73, 77, 80
orthodoxies 38–44, 51

Parkin, F. 15
Parsons, T. 8–12, 51, 53, 100
Pounder, D. 41–42
power approach 12
professional: association 4, 16, 98; judgement 66–67, 72
professionalisation 1, 3, 7; project 3, 97; strategy 54–55
professionalism 2, 15, 17, 19, 53
profession definitions: everyday 1; organisational 2, 16; sociological 2, 7
Propp, V. 85

recruitment 39, 45, 48, 74, 82; see also selection of candidates
regime of practice 25–27, 36, 39
regulation 67, 70–71, 76
responsibility 27, 55–56, 63–64, 74
results 49–51, 54
Robinson, V. 2, 29, 48, 75

science 21–24, 28–30, 35–36
Scribner, S.P. 80–81
selection of candidates 13, 44–45
sensemaking 79, 93, 102
Spillane, J.P. 28–29, 58
standardisation 46–47, 51, 56
standards 22–23, 29–47, 50–51, 56–59

theory movement 24, 35, 98–99
trait analysis 7–12
trust 58, 61–62

Uljens, M. 34, 48
Utdanningsforbundet 1, 55

values: altruism 8, 16, 80; bildung 4, 53, 65; democracy 9, 50, 80; equality 9, 55, 80; service 8, 11, 18

Weber, M. 2, 12–14; see also Neo-Weberians
Weick, K.W. 79, 93
Weinberg, M. 57
welfare state 2, 55, 67, 82
Whiteman, R.S. 38–39, 44
Witz, A. 15–16

Young, M.D. 39, 41

For Product Safety Concerns and Information please contact our EU
representative GPSR@taylorandfrancis.com
Taylor & Francis Verlag GmbH, Kaufingerstraße 24, 80331 München, Germany

www.ingramcontent.com/pod-product-compliance
Lightning Source LLC
Chambersburg PA
CBHW070556170426
43201CB00012B/1855